Granulated Sugar
(caster sugar)

¼ cup = 55g = 4 tbsp
75g   = 6 tbsp
⅓ cup   = 90g
½ cup   = 120g
¾ cup   = 175g
1 cup   = 225g
1¼ cups = 275g
1½ cups = 350g
2 cups   = 450g

Confectioner's Sugar
(icing sugar)

¼ cup   = 25g
½ cup   = 55g
1 cup   = 120g
1½ cups = 175g
1¾ cups = 225g

Flour

¼ cup   = 25g
½ cup   = 55g
⅓ cup   = 75g
¾ cup   = 100g
1 cup   = 120g
1¼ cups = 145g
1½ cups = 175g
1¾ cups = 200g
2 cups   = 225g
2¼ cups = 250g
2½ cups = 275g
3 cups   = 350g
3½ cups = 400g
4 cups   = 450g
4¼ cups = 500g
6½cups = 750g

1 cup   = 225g cream cheese
¾ cup   = 55g grated Parmesan
1 cup   = 85g grated Parmesan
½ cup   = 125g yogurt or sour cream
¾ cup   = 175g yogurt or sour cream
1 cup   = 250g yogurt or sour cream
½ cup   = 115g mayonnaise
1 cup   = 225g mayonnaise

Breadcrumbs

1 cup   = 65g dried
2 cups   = 130g dried
4 cups   = 250g dried
1 cup   = 55g fresh

Dry Ingredients

1 cup   = 225g rice
1 cup   = 200g rolled oats
¼ cup   = 40g ground almonds
¼ cup   = 25g sliced almonds
1 cup   = 150g peanuts
1 cup   = 120g chopped nuts
¾ cup   = 75g cornmeal
1 cup   = 150g raisins
1 cup   = 250g dried beans
2 cups   = 500g dried beans

Hostess with the Mostess

Caroline Barty

Hostess with the Mostess

a galaxy of *retro recipes*

Caroline Barty

MQP

Published by MQ Publications Limited
12 The Ivories
6-8 Northampton Street
London N1 2HY
Tel: +44 (0)20 7359 2244
Fax: +44 (0)20 7359 1616
email: mail@mqpublications.com
website: www.mqpublications.com

Text: Copyright © 2002 Caroline Barty
Editor: Yvonne Deutch
Design: Lindsey Johns, Design Revolution

ISBN: 1-84072-470-6

10 9 8 7 6 5 4 3 2 1

Printed and bound in China

10 simply divine dinner parties

classy canapé parties 104

contents

Introduction

"You're welcome!" A big smile and a cheery greeting vividly convey the generous spirit of home entertaining in the 1950s. Having folks over for a meal or a party was both a pleasure and a challenge for the typical homemaker of the period. Like the hostesses in the following pages, she really enjoyed offering good, old-fashioned hospitality. Inviting friends in for a celebration? What a great idea! There could be no finer way of expressing her pride in her home and family.

This was the decade when, typically, the guys went to work to bring home the bacon, and women stayed at home cooking it. So, women had plenty of time—the magic ingredient that is so often missing from our lives now. That's why *Hostess with the Mostess* is perfectly designed to cater to modern needs. Once you've mastered a few of these tried and tested menus, you'll be entertaining your guests with sweet-tempered poise. In addition, by using the following tips, you can also convey that deliciously indefinable sense of 'time to spare' that characterized the retro years.

Invitations

Unless the occasion is distinctly formal, most of us use e-mail or the telephone; but there's still something very special about getting an invitation through the mail. You could contact prospective guests by phone or e-mail to discuss mutually convenient dates, then mail them a follow-up invitation. It really doesn't have to be stiffly formal—a kind note on a pretty postcard will be much appreciated.

Ambience

Your aim is to make everyone feel comfortable and welcome. Think of the evening as your private theater of pleasure, mutual entertainment, and goodwill. There are several 'props' you can use to achieve an inviting ambience, and these all help to put your guests in a nicely serene, conversational mood.

Polish and perfume

Make sure that your home is clean and shining. Using old-fashioned sweet-smelling beeswax polish on all your wood surfaces will achieve two positive effects—a lovely sheen on the wood and a delicious perfume in the air. A subtle background scent is highly pleasurable, bowls of sweetly scented pot pourri or dried lavender are pretty and delicate in their impact. Some people like to use a few drops of a favorite pure essential oil (lavender, rose, neroli, or jasmine are a few examples) dissolved in tepid water. Decant this into a clean plant spray, and walk through your rooms wafting scented mists into the air shortly before guests arrive. Your home will smell utterly divine.

Atmospheric lighting

Clever lighting can transform the atmosphere of a room, and guests love sitting in intimate pools of soft light where they can quietly relax and unwind. Strategic arrangements of table lamps, uplighters and downlighters are all useful in helping to achieve this; however, for sheer impact, why not banish electric light completely, and light the entire room with candles? Candlelight has a powerfully soothing effect on stressed spirits, so use it generously; candles look fabulous in grouped arrangements, in candelabras and in wall sconces. And, at floor level, bowls of floating candles add a touch of fairytale magic.

Tableware

A white linen tablecloth and matching napkins gives a feeling of cool, clean, crisp refinement to the most ordinary dining table. Keep it freshly washed, starched and ironed. If you're on a budget, look around thrift stores and antique shops—and pounce on any good quality china, linen, glassware, napkin rings, and silverware that you discover. Cleaned and polished, they'll gleam in the soft candlelight of your dinner table.

Flowers

You don't have to fill your home with massed vases of flowers to make an impact; one exquisite, dramatic arrangement situated under a spotlight for glamor lighting will do the trick. And if they're positioned in front of a mirror, so much the better.

Relax

Finally, be ready to greet people at least fifteen minutes before they are due. This will give you plenty of time to get yourself into a welcoming mood; so, when the first guests arrive, they'll know that you're genuinely delighted to have them in your home.

simply divine dinner parties

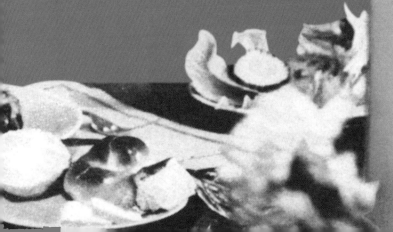

✔ A clean, crisp linen tablecloth, matching napkins, candles, cutlery, wine and water glasses, salt and pepper holders are all the basics you need for arranging a tasteful and welcoming dinner table that would do credit to the smartest hostess of the 1950s.

✔ Try not to use over elaborate settings, they will make your table look cluttered and complicated.

A welcoming dinner table

As you wait for your dinner guests to arrive, you're probably full of anticipation. Everything is gleaming and calm, there's soft music playing, and you've made your home beautifully welcoming and pleasant. But is your dinner table equally inviting? It will be if you follow a few simple guidelines:

✔ Always remember that people are sitting at your table to enjoy each other's company, not to gaze at ornate, towering decorations, so make sure that there is plenty of eye-contact space.

✔ Using candles? Avoid placing them in tall holders that obstruct your guests' view of people sitting opposite. A line of low, squat candles set in individual dishes, and decorated with pretty garlands of fresh flowers will look utterly enchanting, and won't get in the way.

✔ If you want to include an arrangement of fresh flowers, make sure it is in scale with the overall setting, and doesn't dominate the table.

✔ Silverware should be impeccably clean, shining and polished. When arranging it, work from the outside in. For instance, you may want to arrange a setting for a simple meal of soup, meat and salad, and a dessert.

✔ The dinner plate is set one inch from the edge of the table, with the dinner knife placed blade facing inward on the inside right, and a soup spoon to its right. The dinner fork is placed on the left of the plate. Glasses are placed directly above the dinner knife.

✔ The butter knife is normally placed next to the soup spoon on the inside, but it can be placed on the small bread plate. Bread and butter plates sit to the left of the dinner plate.

✔ If you're serving the salad as a separate course, place a second, smaller fork to the left of the large fork. Finally, put a small dessert fork and spoon horizontally across the top of plate, to complete the setting.

✔ Linen napkins look best. If you are not using napkin rings, the table napkin is simply folded in half and placed next to the fork with the crease facing away. If you want to experiment with different folding techniques there are lots of ideas on the internet—just type 'how to fold table napkins' into your search engine, and take your pick.

Mary Lou Owen's
dinner party menu

- Cream of wild mushroom soup
- Roast rib of beef with caramelized shallots
- Duchesse potatoes
- Pear and almond tart with Vanilla cream

Serves 6

Cream of wild mushroom soup

This is a simply luscious soup—and the compliments will all be flowing in your direction. Just nod serenely, and don't mention how ridiculously easy it is to make.

Preparation 20 minutes
Cooking 40 minutes

4 tbsp (55g) butter
1 onion, finely chopped
1 garlic clove, finely chopped
1lb (450g) mixed wild mushrooms, such as girolle, chanterelle, and morels
2oz (55g) white bread, crusts removed
3 tbsp dry sherry
5 cups (1.2lt) chicken or vegetable stock
1 cup (250ml) milk
1 tbsp chopped fresh thyme
½ cup (125ml) heavy (double) cream
1 tbsp chopped fresh parsley
salt and pepper
fried bread croûtons, to serve

1 Melt the butter in a large saucepan, add the onion and garlic and cook for 10 minutes. Add the mushrooms and cook for another 10 minutes.

2 Soak the bread for a few seconds in a little water, squeeze out, and add to the saucepan with the sherry, stock, milk, and thyme. Bring to a boil, then turn the heat down and simmer for 20 minutes. Let cool a little, then stir in the cream.

3 Purée the soup in a blender until very smooth. Taste and season with salt and pepper. Just before serving, stir in the parsley and scatter the croûtons over.

COOK'S TIP
Can't get fresh wild mushrooms? No problem! Try using a mixture of cultivated and dried wild varieties instead.

Roast rib of beef with caramelized shallots

This choice of cut shows that you're a very savvy cook. Did you know that rib has a superior flavor to fillet? If not, you'll be pleasantly surprised! And it's so much more economical. Serve with creamy duchesse potatoes.

Preparation 30 minutes
Cooking 1¾ hours

6lb (2.75kg) rib of beef, bone in
2 tbsp dripping or oil
6 sprigs fresh thyme
1lb (450g) shallots, peeled and left whole
2 tbsp granulated sugar

For the sauce:
1 tbsp all-purpose flour
1 cup (250ml) red wine
2 cups (500ml) good beef stock
salt and pepper

1 Place the beef in a large roasting pan and spoon over the dripping or oil. Season well with salt and pepper and lay the thyme sprigs over the joint. Roast in a preheated oven, 200°C/400°F, Gas 6, for 1 hour.

2 Meanwhile, bring a saucepan of water to a boil, add the shallots and simmer for 15 minutes, then drain well.

3 Remove the beef from the oven. Arrange the shallots around the beef. Sprinkle the sugar over the shallots and return to the oven for another 30 minutes, basting and turning the shallots after 15 minutes. Remove the beef and shallots onto a warm plate and let rest for at least 15 minutes.

4 For the sauce: pour off all but 2 tbsp dripping from the roasting pan, add the flour and cook over the stove for 1–2 minutes. Add the wine, stirring well to prevent lumps, then increase the heat a little and boil the liquid for 3–4 minutes to reduce and thicken.

5 Add the beef stock, reduce the heat and simmer for 10 minutes. Taste and season with salt and pepper.

Duchesse potatoes

Preparation 35 minutes **Cooking** 45 minutes

2lb (1.2kg) maincrop potatoes, peeled
* and halved*
4 tbsp (55g) butter, plus extra for brushing
½ cup (125ml) milk
2 egg yolks

1 Boil the potatoes in salted water until tender, then drain well and mash. Heat the butter and milk in a saucepan and pour the mixture over the potatoes. Beat for a couple of minutes with an electric whisk. Let cool, then mix in the egg yolks.

2 Spoon the mashed potatoes into a piping bag fitted with a wide ridged nozzle and pipe out 18 rosettes on a baking sheet. Melt the remaining butter, brush each rosette, then cook in a preheated oven, 200°C/400°F, Gas 6, for 20 minutes.

Pear and almond tart

For your grand finale, this rich, buttery tart is something of a show-stopper. Serve it with the delicately flavored vanilla cream.

Preparation 40 minutes, plus 30 minutes chilling **Cooking** 1 hour, 20 minutes

2¹⁄₂ cups (275g) all-purpose flour
2 tbsp (25g) confectioners' (icing) sugar,
  plus extra for dusting
3 sticks (350g) unsalted butter, cut into
  cubes
2 egg yolks
4 tbsp ice water
³⁄₄ cup (175g) granulated sugar
1¹⁄₂ cups (175g) ground almonds
2 eggs
a few drops almond extract (optional)
8 pear halves (about 1 can)
¹⁄₄ cup (25g) sliced almonds

1 Mix the flour and confectioners' sugar together in a large bowl and rub in half of the butter. Whisk the egg yolks with 4 tbsp ice water.

2 Make a well in the center of the flour and pour in the egg mixture. Gradually bring the mixture together with a narrow spatula or your hands to form a smooth ball of pastry. Wrap in plastic wrap (cling film) and chill for 30 minutes.

3 Roll out the pastry to line a 9¹⁄₂ in (24cm) loose-bottomed tart pan. Line with baking paper and weigh down with baking beans. Bake in a preheated oven, 190°C/375°F, Gas 5, for 20 minutes or until golden and crisp. Remove the baking paper and beans, then reduce the oven to 180°C/350°F, Gas 4.

4 Cream the remaining butter and granulated sugar until pale and fluffy, then mix in the ground almonds. Gradually whisk in the eggs and the almond extract, if using. Spoon the mixture into the pastry case and level out. Arrange the pear halves on top, pressing them down lightly. Scatter over the sliced almonds.

5 Bake the tart for 55–60 minutes. Remove from the oven and let cool for 10 minutes. Dust with confectioners' sugar just before serving.

COOK'S TIP
Canned pears are used here but use fresh, poached pear halves, if that's easier.

Vanilla cream

Preparation 10 minutes plus
1 hour chilling
Cooking 10 minutes

1 cup (250ml) milk
1 vanilla bean, split
4 egg yolks
4 tbsp (55g) granulated sugar
1 cup (250ml) heavy (double) cream

1 Bring the milk to a boil with the vanilla bean. Beat the egg yolks and granulated sugar together, pour them over the hot milk, then return to the saucepan and stir over a very low heat until the mixture starts to thicken. Let cool, then scrape out the seeds from the vanilla bean and stir into the cold cream. Chill until ready to serve.

Mrs Amy Jackson's
evening supper

- **Tomato and shrimp aspic ring**
- **Veal Cordon Bleu**
- **Crème brûlée with lemon and lime shorties**

Serves 6

Tomato and shrimp aspic ring

Launch the dinner party with a touch of dramatic, scarlet color. This tasty starter was a true retro favorite, and is now making its comeback. Made with shrimp (prawns) combined with a tangy tomato sauce, it is set in a ring mold. Serve with melba toast and a few salad leaves.

Preparation 10 minutes, plus 3–5 hours chilling
Cooking 10 minutes

3¾ cups (900ml) tomato juice
juice of 1 lemon
1 tsp Tabasco sauce
1 tsp celery salt
1 tsp granulated sugar
½ cup (125ml) heavy (double) cream
8 leaves gelatin or 2 tbsp
 granulated gelatin
1lb (450g) cooked, peeled shrimp (prawns)
2 tbsp chopped fresh parsley
oil, for greasing
1 tbsp chopped fresh chives

1 Pour the tomato juice into a large saucepan and add the lemon juice, Tabasco sauce, celery salt, sugar, and cream. Slowly heat until it just reaches simmering point, then take off the heat.

2 Soak the gelatin leaves in cold water for 5 minutes, then squeeze dry. Add to the tomato mixture and stir until completely dissolved. Let chill until the mixture is cold and thick but not set. Stir in the shrimp (prawns) and parsley.

3 Lightly oil a 2pt (1.2lt) ring mold and pour in the tomato and shrimp (prawn) mixture. Stir to distribute the shrimp (prawns) evenly. Cover and chill for at least 3 hours.

4 To remove the mold, place it in a sink of hot water for 10 seconds. Invert onto a serving plate and shake slightly to loosen the sides.

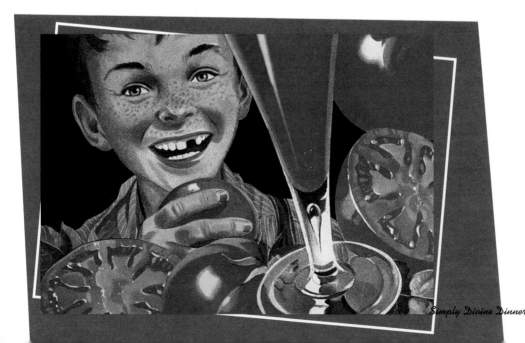

Veal Cordon Bleu

Yes, ma'am! This is so simple, but utterly delicious. The mellow flavor of the veal makes a perfect marriage with the salty ham and melted cheese. Serve this classic dish with wedges of lemon and deep fried parsley.

Preparation 20 minutes
Cooking 16–24 minutes

6 escalopes veal
6 thin slices lean ham
6 thin slices Emmental cheese
1/2 cup (55g) seasoned flour
2 eggs, beaten
2 cups (130g) dried bread crumbs
oil, for shallow frying

1 Place the veal between 2 sheets of plastic wrap (cling film) and flatten with a rolling pin to a thickness of 1/8in (3mm). Lay out on a board.

2 Trim the ham to fit neatly over each veal escalope. Lay a slice of cheese over the ham. Dip each escalope in the seasoned flour, followed by the egg, and finally coat in bread crumbs. Repeat for all the veal escalopes.

3 Heat some oil in a large frying pan and cook 2–3 escalopes at a time for about 4 minutes each side.

COOK'S TIP
Make sure the oil is hot enough before you start frying or the bread crumb crust will become soggy.

Crème brûlée with lemon and lime shorties

Everyone loves crème brûlée! It has got to be one of the best puddings ever. There's nothing nicer than the sound of a teaspoon cracking through the caramelized sugar. The tangy shorties contrast with the rich creaminess of the custard. Simply yummy.

Preparation 20 minutes, plus 3½ hours chilling
Cooking 1 hour 10 minutes

2½ cups (600ml) heavy (double) cream
1 vanilla bean, split
6 egg yolks
3 tbsp granulated sugar
1½ cups (175g) confectioners' (icing) sugar, sifted

For the shorties:
1 cup (120g) all-purpose flour
4 tbsp (55g) cornstarch
4 tbsp (55g) granulated sugar
grated peel of 1 lemon and 1 lime
½ cup(120g) unsalted butter

1 Heat the cream with the vanilla bean until it reaches boiling point. Whisk the egg yolks with the granulated sugar and pour the mixture over the hot cream.

2 Stir the mixture over a low heat until it thickens enough to coat the back of a wooden spoon. Strain into a pitcher, then pour into six ramekins.

3 Stand the ramekins in a roasting pan half full of water and cook in a preheated oven, 150°C/300°F, Gas 2, for 1 hour. Let cool, then chill for at least 3 hours. Just before serving, dust thickly with the confectioners' sugar. Place the ramekins under a preheated broiler (grill) for 3–4 minutes until the sugar caramelizes. Let chill for 30 minutes.

4 Make the shorties while the crème brûlées are baking: mix together the flour, cornstarch, sugar, and lemon and lime peel. Rub in the butter, then bring the crumbs together to form a smooth ball. Roll out onto a lightly floured surface and stamp out 12–14 rounds with a 3in (7.5cm) cookie cutter.

5 Place on a nonstick cookie sheet and cook in a preheated oven, 170°C/325°F, Gas 3, for 20 minutes until golden. Let cool until crisp and store in an airtight container until ready to serve.

COOK'S TIP
You can add scraped vanilla pods to an airtight canister of confectioners' sugar to make vanilla-scented sugar. This is perfect for sprinkling over pastries and cakes.

Bebe Carter's
special supper

- **Smoked trout terrine with cucumber salad**

- **Beef Stroganoff**

- **Dark chocolate and toffee tart**

Serves 6

Smoked trout terrine with cucumber salad

Oh so elegant! The fresh flavor of the cucumber salad cuts through the richness of the smoked trout terrine.

Preparation 25 minutes, plus 3–4 hours chilling
Cooking 10 minutes

2 tbsp (25g) butter
1/4 cup (25g) all-purpose flour
1 1/4 cups (300ml) milk
3 tsp fresh grated horseradish or good
   quality horseradish sauce
1 1/2 cups (350g) mayonnaise
13oz (375g) cooked smoked trout fillets,
   skinned
juice of 1 lemon
4 sheets gelatin or 1 tbsp granulated gelatin
2 egg whites

For the cucumber salad:
1 cucumber, very thinly sliced
2 tbsp white wine vinegar
1 tbsp chopped fresh dill
salt and pepper

1 Melt the butter in a saucepan, stir in the flour and cook for 2–3 minutes. Slowly add the milk, beating to form a smooth, thick sauce. Add the horseradish and season with salt and pepper. Let cool for 15 minutes, then stir in the mayonnaise. Flake the trout into the mayonnaise mixture.

2 Mix the lemon juice with 5–6 tbsp cold water in a small saucepan and soak the gelatin for 5 minutes. Heat the gelatin until it has dissolved. Pour into the mousse mixture and mix well.

3 Whisk the egg whites to soft peaks and fold into the smoked trout mixture. Spoon into a 2pt (1.2lt) terrine, which has been lined with plastic wrap (cling film). Cover and let chill for 3–4 hours.

4 For the cucumber salad: place the cucumber in a shallow bowl. Pour the white wine vinegar over and stir in the dill. Season with black pepper.

5 To serve, invert the terrine onto a plate and serve in slices, accompanied by the cucumber salad.

COOK'S TIP
If you want, you can serve the terrine as a pâté with warm toast, in which case spoon it into a soufflé dish instead of setting it in a terrine mold.

Beef Stroganoff

A timeless classic, this will take pride of place on your table and evoke appreciative murmurs of pleasure from your dinner guests. This is a good dish to add to your repertoire for future memorable occasions. Serve with boiled rice and a salad.

Preparation 35 minutes
Cooking 30 minutes

4 tbsp (55g) butter
2 tbsp oil
1 onion, finely sliced
3lb (1.5kg) fillet of beef, cut into long, thin slices
3 tbsp brandy
1 cup (250ml) white wine
1½ lb (675g) large mushrooms, finely sliced
½ tsp grated nutmeg
1 cup (250ml) heavy (double) cream
1 tbsp lemon juice
salt and pepper

1 Heat half the butter and oil in a large frying pan and cook the onion for 10 minutes until soft and golden. Remove to a large bowl.

2 Heat the remaining butter and oil in the frying pan and sear the beef over a very high heat, 2–3 handfuls at a time, for 1 minute. Remove and mix with the onions while you continue to cook the rest of the beef. Set aside.

3 Add the mushrooms to the frying pan and cook over a high heat for 5 minutes until tender.

4 Return the beef and onions to the frying pan and mix with the mushrooms. Add the brandy and white wine, then increase the heat and cook until the liquid has reduced by half. Season with salt, pepper, and nutmeg.

5 Mix the cream with the lemon juice and add to the frying pan, then heat through before serving.

COOK'S TIP
The secret to the success of this dish is not to overcook the beef, as the fillet is the most tender cut and requires very little cooking. So, be a well organized hostess and prepare all the ingredients before you start.

Dark chocolate and toffee tart

As a final flourish, wow your guests with this rich, frankly indulgent, tart. It's pure pleasure served with a spoonful of luscious cream.

Preparation 45 minutes, plus 3 hours chilling
Cooking 40 minutes

2½ cups (275g) all-purpose flour
¼ cup (25g) confectioners' (icing) sugar
1½ sticks (175g) unsalted butter, in cubes
2 egg yolks
2 cups (350g) granulated sugar
½ cup (150g) golden or corn syrup
½ cup (120g) unsalted butter
1 cup (250ml) heavy (double) cream
1 tsp vanilla extract
½ cup (120g) unsalted butter
½ cup (120g) dark chocolate, grated

1 Mix the flour and confectioners' sugar together in a large bowl and rub in the butter. Whisk the egg yolks with 4 tbsp very cold water. Make a well in the center of the flour and pour in the egg mixture.

2 Bring the mixture together with a spatula or your hands to form a smooth ball. Wrap in plastic wrap (cling film) and chill for 30 minutes.

3 Roll out the pastry to line a 9½ in (24cm) loose-bottomed tart pan. Line with baking paper and weigh down with baking beans. Bake in a preheated oven, 190°C/375°F, Gas Mark 5, for 20 minutes or until golden and crisp. Remove the baking paper and beans.

4 Place ½ cup (125ml) water in a large saucepan. Add the sugar and syrup and cook over a low heat until the sugar has dissolved. Increase the heat and bubble for about 10 minutes, until the sauce is a deep caramel colour.

5 Add the butter, cream, and vanilla extract and stand back—it will bubble up. Stir until the mixture is smooth. Pour into the pastry case and chill for 2 hours until set and firm.

6 Melt the chocolate with the butter in a bowl placed over barely simmering water. Let stand for 15 minutes, then pour the chocolate mixture over the top of the tart, spreading it evenly with a narrow spatula. Let set in the refrigerator for at least 1 hour before serving.

Mrs Beth Wilson's
first choice dinner

- **Home-cured gravadlax**

- **Warm potato cakes**

- **Rosemary lamb with anchovy butter**

- **Baked lemon custards with brandy snaps**

Serves 6

28

Home-cured gravadlax

Here's your chance to learn a special art! If you've never cured your own salmon, this will be a revelation. And your guests will all agree that it's far superior to any store-bought gravadlax. Delicious with warm potato cakes.

Preparation 20 minutes, plus 30 minutes chilling and 24 hours curing
Cooking 15 minutes

3 tbsp fine rock salt
2 tbsp granulated sugar
3 tbsp chopped fresh dill
1½ lb (675g) salmon fillet

For the sauce:
2 tbsp Dijon mustard
2 tbsp soft brown sugar
3 tbsp chopped fresh dill
6 tbsp oil

1 Mix together the salt, sugar, and dill and sprinkle half into a dish large enough for the salmon. Place the salmon in the dish, skin side down, and sprinkle over the remaining salt mixture. Cover with plastic wrap (cling film) and weigh the fish down. Let chill for 12 hours, then turn the fish over and replace the weights. Let chill for another 12 hours.

2 To make the sauce: place the mustard, sugar, and dill in a blender and pour in the oil. Process until the sauce amalgamates and thickens. Spoon into a bowl, cover and chill until ready to serve.

3 Before serving, remove the salmon from the marinade and pat dry. Thinly slice the salmon and lay a couple of slices onto each potato cake. Finally, spoon over a little dill and mustard sauce.

COOK'S TIP
Remember to start preparing the salmon at least 24 hours in advance of serving.

Warm potato cakes

Preparation 25 minutes **Cooking** 20 minutes

2lb (900g) maincrop potatoes, peeled and
* roughly grated*
1 tbsp chopped fresh chives
2 eggs, beaten
⅓ cup (75g) self-rising flour
4 tbsp oil
salt and pepper

1 Lay a clean dish towel in a large bowl, spoon in the grated potatoes, then bring the ends of the towel together and squeeze out the liquid starch.

2 Return the potatoes to the clean bowl and add the chives, eggs, and flour, and season well with salt and pepper. Shape the potato mixture into 6 large cakes.

3 Heat the oil in a large, nonstick frying pan and drop in the potato cakes. Cook each cake for 4–5 minutes per side.

Rosemary lamb with anchovy butter

Fragrant and meltingly moist, this lamb roast has an exquisite flavor. Serve with crisp roast potatoes and seasonal vegetables.

Preparation 40 minutes, plus 30 minutes chilling
Cooking 25 minutes

8 anchovy fillets in oil, drained
3/4 cup (175g) softened butter
4 x 12oz (350g) best end fillets of lamb
8 large sprigs fresh rosemary
2 tbsp oil
1 tsp Dijon mustard
salt and pepper

1 Pound the anchovies in a mortar to a smooth paste. Place the softened butter in a bowl and beat in the anchovy paste, followed by the mustard. Shape the butter into a cylinder, wrap in plastic wrap (cling film) and chill until firm. Unwrap and cut into 6 disks. Let chill until ready to serve.

2 Lay the lamb fillets on a board and place 2 rosemary sprigs on each one. Tie up each fillet with string. Season the meat with salt and pepper and place in a roasting pan.

3 Pour the oil over and roast in a preheated oven, 200°C/400°F, Gas 6, for 20–25 minutes. Let rest for 5 minutes.

4 Before serving, remove the string and rosemary and slice the lamb into about 6 pieces per fillet. Serve the lamb with a disk of anchovy butter.

COOK'S TIP

Make sure you buy the best end lamb fillet, as it is the leanest, most tender joint. Don't get it confused with neck fillet which is fattier and best suited to casseroles.

Baked lemon custards with brandy snaps

These light, citrus-flavored, individual baked custards are a traditional favorite—and, even better, they're a breeze to make.

Preparation 30 minutes, plus 4 hours chilling
Cooking 1 hour, 10 minutes

2½ cups (600ml) heavy (double) cream
8 egg yolks
1½ cups (175g) confectioners' (icing)
 sugar, sifted
juice of 4 lemons

For the brandy snaps:
½ cup (120g) butter, plus extra for greasing
½ cup (120g) granulated sugar
4 tbsp golden or corn syrup
1 cup (120g) flour
juice of 1 lemon
pinch of ground ginger

1 Mix the first 4 ingredients together and pour into 6 ramekins. Half-fill a roasting pan with hot water and place the ramekins in the pan. Cook in a preheated oven, 150°C/300°F, Gas 2, for 1 hour. Remove and let chill for 4 hours.

2 For the brandy snaps: grease a large baking sheet and the handles of 6 wooden spoons or something of a similar size.

3 Melt the butter, sugar, and golden syrup in a saucepan. Remove from the heat and stir in the flour, lemon juice, and ground ginger.

4 Place teaspoons of the mixture on the baking sheet, making sure you leave a gap of at least 6in (15cm) as the mixture spreads during cooking. Bake in a preheated oven, 190°C/375°F, Gas 5, for 5–6 minutes until golden brown. Set aside the brandy snaps for a few minutes until cool enough to handle. Shape each one around the handle of a wooden spoon.

5 When cold and crisp, slip the brandy snaps off the handles and store in an airtight container until ready to serve with the custards.

COOK'S TIP
Check that you have enough cream before pouring it into the ramekins—if the lemons have yielded little juice, you may want to add extra.

cool, elegant lunches

A little light luncheon

There's an irresistible connection between the idea of a lunch party and the image of 'ladies who lunch.' It conjures up memories from a more leisurely era, of course. During the 1950s, roles were more stereotyped. Men were the ones who went out to work, while most women were full-time home-makers. Women had much more time to get to know their neighbors, and often invited each other over for a friendly lunch.

Lunch parties were also natural ways of bringing together women who belonged to social groups such as bridge clubs, charity committees and various other community organizations. Some still do all this, of course, but it's increasingly the case that modern women are more likely to have business lunches during the working day, or, more often, a quick sandwich eaten at the desk.

✔ If this is typical of your day, it doesn't mean that hostessing lunch parties is out of the question. You simply have to move the occasion to the weekend, when you know that your guests are more likely to have time to come over to your place during the day. Sunday is a good choice, because everyone has had time to wind down the day before, and feel more relaxed.

✔ In fact, relaxation should be the keynote theme in your mind when you're planning a lunch party. The event should make a calming, pleasurable break in the day—especially when the weather's good and the lunch table is bathed in sunlight.

✔ Some of the nicest lunch parties are held outdoors; they can be set in the garden, on your porch, patio, balcony or terrace, or in a well-lit conservatory. If you don't have an outdoor space, pick the lightest, brightest spot that you can find in your home, and set your lunch table there.

✔ The menus featured in the following pages are all perfectly devised to be cool and elegant; they also have a simple charm. You can reflect that mood in your presentation; lunch tables should have an engaging prettiness and lightness of touch in contrast to the formality of dinner party settings.

✔ If you normally opt for classic white table linen for dinner parties, try dressing your lunch table in delicate pastels, or strong, vibrant colors for a change? Both look great in natural light.

✔ Add even more color with decorative china and fresh flowers. And, if you own an informal cutlery set with colorful perspex handles (they come in rainbow colors of red, blue, green, yellow, and purple) why not display them at lunch?

✔ What to wear? If you want uphold your reputation as 'the hostess with the mostess' make sure you dress the part. The chic 50s hostess would have chosen a sleek sheath, simple chemise, or crisp shirtwaster. Her aim was to achieve a sense of effortless chic. You can do likewise—the secret is, wear something stylishly informal, and you'll be able to relax and entertain your lunch guests with confidence.

Mrs Brett Martin's
simple summer lunch

- **Egg and shrimp mayonnaise**
- **Sirloin of beef with tomato and sour cream salad**

Serves 6

Egg and shrimp mayonnaise

This light starter always brings back happy memories of perfect summer lunch parties. A true classic, it's at its very best when made with good quality shrimp (prawns).

Preparation 25 minutes
Cooking 20 minutes

6 eggs
salad leaves
12oz (350g) cooked, peeled shrimp (prawns)
1 tbsp chopped fresh chives, to garnish

For the mayonnaise:
1 red bell pepper, halved and seeded
1 egg, plus 1 egg yolk
1 tsp mustard powder
2 tsp white wine vinegar
3–4 drops Tabasco sauce
1¼ cups (300ml) sunflower oil
salt and pepper

1 Boil the eggs for 8 minutes, cool under cold running water and when cold peel off the shell. Set aside.

2 For the mayonnaise: place the pepper on a baking sheet, cut side down, and broil (grill) for 10 minutes until the skin is charred. Place in a plastic freezer bag and leave until cold, then peel off the skin.

3 Place the egg and egg yolk in a food processor with the mustard powder, white wine vinegar, and Tabasco sauce and blend until smooth. Keep the motor running while you slowly pour in the oil. When the mayonnaise is thick and emulsified, add the bell pepper and process until smooth. Taste and season with salt and pepper.

4 Take 6 glass bowls and place some salad leaves in the bottom of each one. Quarter the hard-cooked eggs and arrange over the salad leaves. Pile the shrimp (prawns) on top and spoon over 2 tbsp mayonnaise. Garnish with chives.

Sirloin of beef with tomato and sour cream salad

For understated elegance, what could be more satisfying than top quality, cold roast beef, cooked to perfection. All it needs for an accompaniment is some fresh, crusty bread and a green salad.

Preparation 20 minutes
Cooking 50–60 minutes

3lb (1.5kg) sirloin of beef
2 garlic cloves, crushed
1 tsp dried rosemary
6 ripe beef tomatoes
1 cup (250ml) sour cream
grated peel of 1 lemon
2 tbsp chopped fresh chives
salt and pepper

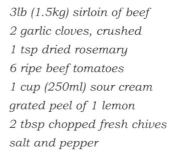

1 Place the beef in a roasting pan and smear over the garlic and rosemary. Season well with salt and pepper. Cook in a preheated oven, 200°C/400°F, Gas 6, for 50–60 minutes, depending on the thickness of the joint. Remove from the oven and let cool.

2 Place the tomatoes in a large bowl and pour boiling water over them. Leave for 20 seconds, then drain and refresh under cold running water. Pat dry and peel off the skins. Thinly slice the tomatoes and arrange them in the center of a large serving plate.

3 Mix the sour cream with the lemon rind and season with salt and pepper. Spoon it over the tomatoes and sprinkle with the chives.

4 To serve, thinly slice the beef and arrange around the tomato salad.

Gracie Irwin's special lunch party

- **Roast chicken stuffed with pâté**
- **Summer berry tart**

Serves 6

Roast chicken stuffed with pâté

Want to make an impression? Here's how. True, this dish is quite time consuming to make, but it really is worth the effort. You can use store-bought pâté but there is no substitute for homemade. Serve cold with a mixed leaf salad.

Preparation 40 minutes, plus 24 hours chilling
Cooking 2½ hours

whole 3lb (1.3kg) boned chicken (get your
  butcher to do this)
2 tbsp (25g) softened butter

For the pâté:
1 onion, very finely chopped
1 garlic clove, crushed
4 tbsp (55g) butter
½ cup (125ml) red wine
½ tsp dried mixed herbs
4oz (115g) pig's liver
5oz (150g) chicken livers, trimmed of any
  membranes
4oz (115g) minced pork
4oz (115g) minced raw ham
1 egg
½ cup (125ml) heavy (double) cream
8oz (225g) streaky bacon
salt and pepper

1 To make the pâté: fry the onion and garlic in the butter for 10 minutes. Add the red wine and bring to a boil, then bubble for 5 minutes until the liquid has reduced to about 3 tbsp.

2 Add the mixed herbs, pig's and chicken livers, minced pork, and ham to the pan, then cook gently for 10 minutes. Remove from the heat and season with a little salt and pepper. Let cool and add the egg and cream.

3 Line the bottom and sides of a 2pt (1.2lt) loaf pan with the bacon. Spoon the pâté into the pan, fold over any overlapping bacon and cover with aluminum foil.

4 Place the loaf pan in a roasting tin half full of boiling water and cook in a preheated oven, 150°C/300°F, Gas 2, for 1¼ hours. Remove the pan from the water and weigh down. Let cool and chill overnight.

5 Lay out the boned chicken on a board, skin side down. Scoop out half of the pâté and arrange it in the middle of the chicken. Bring up the sides and fold in the top and bottom and either sew or secure with skewers.

6 Place the chicken, join side down, in a roasting pan and smear the skin with butter. Roast in a preheated oven, 200°C/400°F, Gas 6, for 50 minutes. Let cool, then chill for at least 24 hours. Slice the chicken thinly before serving.

COOK'S TIP
The pâté recipe makes more than is needed, but it will keep for up to a week or can be frozen.

Summer berry tart

This mixed berry tart is so, so pretty, and tastes simply divine. Like you, it's immensely versatile, so you can experiment with different varieties of fruit depending on what is in season. Serve it with a spoonful of cream.

Preparation 40 minutes, plus 1 hour chilling
Cooking 30 minutes

2½ cups (275g) all-purpose flour
4 tbsp (25g) confectioners' sugar
1½ sticks (175g) unsalted butter, in cubes
2 egg yolks

For the filling:
2½ cups (600ml) milk
4 egg yolks
6 tbsp (75g) granulated sugar
¼ cup (25g) all-purpose flour
¼ cup (25g) cornstarch
grated peel of 1 orange
⅔ cup (150ml) heavy (double) cream
1lb (450g) mixed summer berries such as
   raspberries, strawberries, blueberries,
   redcurrants
confectioners' sugar, for dusting

1 Mix together the flour and confectioners' sugar in a large bowl and rub in the butter. Whisk the egg yolks with 4 tbsp cold water. Make a well in the center of the flour and pour in the egg mixture. Gradually bring the mixture together with a narrow spatula or your hands to form a smooth ball of pastry. Wrap in plastic wrap (cling film) and chill for 30 minutes.

2 Roll out the pastry to line a 9½ in (24cm) loose-bottomed tart pan. Line with baking paper and weigh down with baking beans. Bake in a preheated oven, 190°C/375°F, Gas 5, for 20 minutes or until golden and crisp. Remove the baking paper and beans and let cool.

3 To make the filling: pour the milk into a nonstick pan and bring to a boil. Mix the egg yolks with the sugar and stir in the flour and cornstarch. Pour the mixture over the hot milk and mix well.

4 Bring the hot milk mixture to a boil, stirring continuously to prevent lumps forming. Once the custard is thick and smooth, remove from the heat and stir in the orange rind. Cover and let chill.

5 Whip the cream to soft peaks, then fold into the cold custard. Spoon into the pastry case and level off. Arrange the mixed summer fruit over the custard and dust with icing sugar before serving.

Phoebe Dickson's
favorite summer lunch

- Chilled avocado and dill soup with fresh crabmeat

- Home smoked salmon with New England potato salad

Serves 6

Chilled avocado and dill soup with fresh crabmeat

Such style, my dear! On a hot summer's day put your guests in a cool, calm mood with this chilled, luxurious soup.

Preparation 10 minutes, plus 1 hour chilling

3 ripe avocados, pitted and peeled
1 small garlic clove, crushed
juice of ½ lemon
2½ cups (600ml) cold, fresh chicken stock
⅔ cup (150ml) sour cream
2 tbsp finely chopped fresh dill
dash of Tabasco sauce
8oz (225g) fresh white crabmeat
salt and pepper
2 green (spring) onions, finely chopped,
  to garnish

1 Place the avocados, garlic, lemon juice, and stock in a food processor or blender and process until smooth. Pour into a bowl, stir in the sour cream, dill, and Tabasco. Taste and season well with salt and pepper. Let chill for 1 hour.

2 To serve, pour into 6 bowls and flake some crabmeat into the center of each one. Sprinkle over the chopped onions and serve immediately.

COOK'S TIP
Use ripe, buttery soft avocados, and the freshest crabmeat for the finest flavor.

Home smoked salmon with New England potato salad

"How does she manage to do it?" That's what your guests will be asking when they taste this divine dish. Be gracious, and smile quietly as you enjoy the compliments. Serve with a green salad.

Preparation 25 minutes
Cooking 30 minutes

For the potato salad
1½ lb (675g) waxy new potatoes,
  halved if large
3 sticks celery, finely diced
2 green (spring) onions, finely sliced
1 red bell pepper, seeded and finely diced
1 cup (225g) mayonnaise
⅔ cup (150ml) sour cream
2 tbsp chopped fresh parsley
salt and pepper

For the smoked salmon:
1 cup (175g) rice
8 sprigs fresh rosemary
6 x 6oz (175g) salmon fillets
2 tsp oil

1 To make the potato salad: boil the potatoes in salted water for 15–20 minutes until just soft. Drain well and cut into small pieces. Place in a large bowl with the celery, onions, and bell pepper.

2 Mix the mayonnaise with the sour cream and season with salt and pepper, then spoon the mixture over the potato salad. Mix well until all the ingredients are thoroughly coated and lightly stir in the parsley. Let chill until ready to serve.

3 Line a wok with aluminum foil and pour in the rice. Arrange the rosemary over the top of the rice. Sprinkle with a little water and fit a round wire rack in the wok. Heat the wok until smoking, then place the salmon fillets on the wire rack. Cover tightly and smoke for 5 minutes.

4 Remove the salmon to a roasting pan and brush it with oil. Season with salt and pepper and cook in a preheated oven, 200°C/400°F, Gas 6, for 5 minutes. Rest for a few minutes and serve the salmon warm with the potato salad.

COOK'S TIP
If you don't want to smoke the salmon indoors as described, you can prepare it over a barbecue grill.

Mrs Carrie Mason's
informal lunch party

- **Manhattan-style clam chowder**
- **Club sandwiches**
- **Coffee cheesecake with pecan sauce**

Serves 6

Manhattan-style clam chowder

Celebrate your heritage with this time-honored classic—it is
such a great dish for an informal lunch, and makes a
perfect partnership with tasty club sandwiches.

Preparation 25 minutes
Cooking 55 minutes

3 tbsp oil
1 onion, finely chopped
3 sticks celery, finely chopped
1 green bell pepper, seeded and
  finely diced
10oz (275g) potatoes, peeled and
  finely diced
4oz (115g) bacon, diced
14oz (400g) can chopped tomatoes
3 cups (750ml) chicken stock
½ tsp paprika
10oz (275g) shucked (shelled)
  clams
2 tbsp chopped fresh parsley
salt and pepper

1 Heat the oil in a large saucepan and add the
onion, celery, and bell pepper and cook gently for
20 minutes. Add the potatoes, bacon, chopped
tomatoes, chicken stock, and paprika. Bring to a
boil, then reduce the heat and simmer for
30 minutes.

2 Stir in the clams and parsley and simmer for
another 5 minutes. Taste and season with salt
and pepper.

Club sandwiches

A good club sandwich is a miniature masterpiece, and everyone has their favorite recipe. Try mine for size.

Preparation 20 minutes

18 slices white bread
3 large tomatoes, thinly sliced
3 cooked chicken breasts, thinly sliced
6 tbsp mayonnaise, preferably homemade
18 slices bacon, fried until crisp
crisp lettuce leaves
salt and pepper

1 Toast the bread. Lay 6 pieces on a board and top each one with slices of tomato. Pile the sliced chicken on top and season with salt and pepper.

2 Place a second slice of toast over the chicken and spread with the mayonnaise. Lay 3 bacon slices on top of each one and arrange some lettuce leaves over the bacon.

3 Top with the remaining toast, halve the sandwiches diagonally and secure with cocktail sticks.

COOK'S TIP
The ingredients for these club sandwiches are just a suggestion—you can select any fillings of your choice.

Coffee cheesecake with pecan sauce

Have them purring with pleasure with this rich, creamy cheesecake made extra luxurious with a luscious sauce.

Preparation 20 minutes, plus 2 hours, 20 minutes chilling and cooling
Cooking 1 hour 5 minutes

7oz (200g) digestive biscuits
4 tbsp (55g) unsalted butter, melted
2¾ cups (600g) cream cheese
1 cup (200g) soft brown sugar
1 tsp vanilla extract
3 eggs
2 tbsp very strong brewed coffee

For the sauce:
4 tbsp (55g) unsalted butter
6 tbsp (75g) soft brown sugar
1 cup (250ml) heavy (double) cream
1 tsp vanilla extract
¾ cup (75g) pecans, toasted and finely chopped

1 Crush the biscuits into fine bread crumbs and stir in the melted butter. Press into the bottom of an 8in (20cm) springform cake pan and chill for 20 minutes.

2 Beat the cream cheese with the sugar and vanilla extract. Add the eggs and beat until smooth. Stir in the coffee, then spoon the mixture into the cake pan.

3 Place the cake pan in a roasting pan half full of boiling water and cook in a preheated oven, 180°C/350°F, Gas 4, for 55 minutes. Turn off the heat and let the cheesecake cool in the oven for 1 hour. Chill for at least 1 hour in the refrigerator before serving.

4 For the sauce: melt the butter in a small saucepan and add the sugar, cream, and vanilla extract. Simmer for 10 minutes, then stir in the pecans. Serve warm with the cold cheesecake.

Cool, Elegant Lunches

53

Mrs Tammy Redner's
ladies lunch

- **Mushroom and bacon tart with Zucchini salad**

- **Blueberry crumble ice cream**

Serves 6

Mushroom and bacon tart

Love up the ladies with this light, creamy tart. It's really a breeze to make, but delicious nonetheless. Serve it with a tangy, zucchini (courgette) salad.

Preparation 20 minutes
Cooking 55 minutes

2 cups (225g) all-purpose flour
5 tbsp (75g) butter
2tbsp (25g) white vegetable shortening
  (white vegetable fat)

For the filling:
5 tbsp (75g) butter
8oz (225g) portabello mushrooms,
  thinly sliced
4oz (115g) bacon, cut into small pieces
1 cup (225g) cream cheese
3 eggs
½ cup (125g) sour cream
2 tbsp grated cheese such as Cheddar
salt and pepper

1 Place the flour and a pinch of salt in a bowl and rub in the butter and white fat or lard. Add 2–3 tbsp cold water and bring the mixture together with a narrow spatula or your hands to form a smooth ball of pastry. Wrap in plastic wrap (cling film) and chill for 30 minutes.

2 Roll out the pastry to line a 10in (25cm) tart pan. Line with baking paper and weigh down with baking beans. Bake in a preheated oven, 190°C/375°F, Gas 5, for 15–20 minutes or until golden and crisp. Remove the baking paper and beans, then reduce the oven to 170°C/325°F, Gas 3.

3 To make the filling: Melt 2oz (55g) butter in a frying pan and cook the mushrooms for 5 minutes. Remove to a plate and wipe the frying pan with paper towels. Melt the remaining butter and cook the bacon for 5 minutes. Scatter the mushrooms and bacon evenly in the pastry case.

4 Beat the cream cheese with the eggs and sour cream, and season with salt and pepper. Pour the mixture into the pastry case and sprinkle over the cheese. Bake for 20–25 minutes until just set.

Zucchini salad

Preparation 10 minutes
Cooking 40 minutes

2lb (900g) zucchini (courgettes) cut into batons
6 tbsp oil
juice of 1 lemon
3 sprigs fresh rosemary
salt and pepper

1 Toss the zucchini in the oil and lemon juice. Place in a roasting pan with the rosemary. Season with salt and pepper. Roast in a preheated oven, 200°C/400°F, Gas 6, for 35–40 minutes. Remove the rosemary and serve at room temperature.

Blueberry crumble ice cream

Homemade blueberry ice cream—what a delicious treat for your guests! You're a wonderful hostess.

Preparation 45 minutes, plus 3 hours freezing
Cooking 30 minutes

1²⁄₃ cups (400ml) milk
4 egg yolks
4 tbsp (55g) granulated sugar
1 tsp vanilla extract
1¼ cups (300ml) heavy (double) cream

For the crumble:
½ cup (55g) all-purpose flour
4 tbsp (55g) soft brown sugar
4 tbsp (55g) butter

For the blueberry purée:
1¾ cups (225g) blueberries
4 tbsp (55g) granulated sugar

1 Bring the milk to a boil in a large saucepan. Mix the egg yolks with the sugar in a large bowl. Pour the hot milk over the egg yolk mixture, stir well, then return to the pan. Heat gently until the custard starts to thicken slightly.

2 Add the vanilla extract, then remove from the heat, strain into a clean bowl and let cool. Lightly whip the cream and fold into the cool custard.

Ladies who lunch

56

3 Pour the mixture into a shallow container and freeze for 2 hours, then mash with a fork to disperse the ice crystals and return to the freezer for another 1 hour by which stage it should be fairly firm.

4 For the crumble: mix the flour and sugar together and rub in the butter until you have a bread crumb consistency. Spread the crumbs onto a baking sheet and cook in a preheated oven, 200°C/400°F, Gas 6, for 10 minutes. When the crumbs are cool and crisp, break into small pieces.

5 For the purée: place the blueberries and sugar in a saucepan and gently stew for 5 minutes. Purée the fruit in a blender, then pass through a strainer to remove any pips and skin. Let chill.

6 When the ice cream is set, fold in the crumble and then the blueberry purée. Don't overwork it— you want a streaky, rippled effect. Freeze until ready to serve.

COOK'S TIP
This ice cream is quite easy to make, but takes time if you haven't got an ice cream maker. It's best to make it 24 hours in advance of serving.

very
special
occasions

✔ Let your imagination soar

If the very thought makes you go pale with alarm, why not take a look at the menu for a Cowboy Birthday Beano devised by the unflappable Mrs Ginger Bailey? Doesn't that sound like bushels of fun straight out of the mainstream 1950s? Forget about being a cool sophisticate; smile, throw yourself into the spirit of the occasion, and you'll soon discover how quickly your imagination is fired up.

The spirit of the occasion

To be a successful 'hostess with the mostess' you'll need to be a highly versatile person with an excellent sense of humor. Does that description fit you, do you think? OK. So you're already a legend amongst your friends for your oh-so-smart cocktail gatherings; but how do you feel about throwing a rip-roaring birthday bash for a bunch of excited kids?

✔ Honor tradition

Very few of the special occasions featured in the following pages require complicated menus or stiff, formal set-ups. However, they do have one thing in common; they all celebrate much loved traditional events that are important and familiar in most people's lives. Simple but magical occasions such as Halloween, birthday celebrations and college graduation provide abiding memories that are treasured for ever. And all this builds into a shared experience of custom and culture that brings everyone together. When you think about the most vivid moments of your life, you're far more likely to recall dressing up on Halloween night to go out Trick-or-Treating with your best pals from the neighborhood than going off on some exotic foreign trip.

✔Providing hospitality

It's all too easy to become so hypnotized by glitz and glamor, you simply forget how to have fun in your own home. And that's the charm of many of these ideas; for instance, it's important to keep up the tradition of sleepovers and slumber parties, so that your kids learn to make space in their room for their friends. And they'll really appreciate all the thought and effort that you put into hosting these occasions. Meanwhile, what are they getting out of the occasion? Essentially, they are learning the wonderful spirit of hospitality and the knowledge that you can have a great time right there in your own home.

✔Home sweet home

The more you appreciate these classic celebrations from the heart of 1950s life, the more you'll understand why those years can seem like a far off idyll, when everything was simpler and more straightforward. Much of the era's appeal is due to the fact that entertaining was mostly based around the home; the war had ended, fathers and husbands had come back home, and all the values of family life came into focus as never before.

✔The modern hostess

Nowadays, you're just as likely to be trying to survive the ups and downs of your job in addition to running a home; so it's just as well that today's 'hostess with the mostess' can call up a raft of party theme ideas from internet sites and magazines, as well as specialist stores that sell party accessories for all kinds of events. The secret is to choose ideas that appeal to your imagination, so that you can bring all your enthusiasm and energy into play, and add your personal touch to the particular occasion.

✔Get equipped

If you're regularly arranging events such as parties, picnics or barbecues, make sure you have all the equipment you'll need. For instance, keep a checklist of your basic picnic kit, and immediately replace anything that's broken or missing, so you won't be running around on the morning of your departure. Also, do make sure that your barbecue fires up promptly, and that you have all your tools ready at hand.

✔Finally, have fun

Once you've discovered how much pleasure you can get from holding special occasion parties for guests all ages, you'll have found the key to being a good hostess; that is, the ability to enter into the true spirit of the event with real joy.

Joleen Hartwell's teen sleepover special

- **Pasta shells filled with bolognese**
- **Cheese and tomato pizza**
- **Chocolate fondue with marshmallows**

Serves 6

Joleen's friendly sleepover menu encourages teen visitors to fuel up on their favorite foods while they giggle and gossip the night away. They'll specially adore the chocolate fondue, as it's so nice to dip in together.

Sleepover or slumber parties have become a central part of just about every junior citizen's social life. Their popularity is growing, so it's a very good idea to know how to host these events with good humor. Most parents are happy to do so; they know that slumber parties are a great opportunity for young teens to learn how to extend hospitality, and share personal space with their favorite friends.

The following tips will help to make your party special:

✔ Get teen guests in the right mood with cute invitations—traditional 'sleepy' themes always go down well. Look out for themed motifs such as teddy bears, nightgowns, pajamas, slippers, pillows, hair curlers, moon and stars. Anything connected with bedtime does the trick.

✔ As for decorating the sleepover room, you really can't go over the top. Fill it with colorful garlands, balloons, and streamers; and try to create a central focus where everyone can sit comfortably together.

✔ Organize the space so it's easy to share. For instance, they'll be perfectly happy sitting on cushions around a low table. Serve their food on this, so they can all eat close together.

✔ Use the same approach for arranging sleeping bags. After they've finished eating, place their sleeping bags around the center of the room in a starburst layout. Everyone's heads should face in towards the center—this encourages cozy talk and friendliness.

✔ Keep the lights low, and provide a few bowls of yummy snacks such as corn chips, potato chips, pretzels, popcorn, plus a few dips. They'll certainly work up a fiendish appetite with all that talking. Some teens really enjoy having their favorite giant toys scattered around, while

others feel it's too babyish. Depending on the group's whim, they may spend hours on beauty preening, hair curling and nail polishing; or listening to favorite CDs; or telling each other spooky ghost stories. Every group of teens is different.

✔ It's important to set time limits, otherwise you'll be faced with a red-eyed bunch of irritable characters the following morning. Stay diplomatically in the background until 'lights out' then firmly announce when it's time to sleep. Paste some glow-in-the-dark stars on the ceiling to add a touch of magic to the room.

✔ The following morning, keep things simple. They'll be famished again, so arrange a selection of cereals, breads, fruit, butter, milk, and juices on the kitchen table and let them help themselves before they set off for home.

Pasta shells filled with bolognese

The giggles, the screams! Your teen guests will work up quite an appetite with all that excitement. So they'll tuck into this hearty bolognese dish with gusto.

Preparation 20 minutes **Cooking** 1 hour, 55 minutes

2 tbsp oil
1 onion, finely chopped
1 garlic clove, crushed
2 sticks celery,
  finely chopped
2oz (50g) streaky bacon
1lb 10oz (750g) ground beef
3 cups (600g) canned
  chopped tomatoes
3 tbsp tomato purée
1 tsp mixed dried herbs
1²/₃ cups (400ml) milk
1lb 2oz (500g) large dried
  pasta shells
1 tbsp oil
salt and pepper
grated Parmesan, to serve
  (optional)

COOK'S TIP
Large pasta shells are sold in good Italian delis, but you could serve the sauce with spaghetti instead.

1 Heat the oil in a large saucepan, add the onion, garlic, and celery and cook for 10 minutes. Add the bacon and ground beef and cook, stirring, over a high heat for 3–4 minutes until the beef has browned.

2 Stir in the chopped tomatoes, tomato purée, herbs, and 1 cup (250ml) milk. Cover and simmer the bolognese for 40 minutes.

3 Add the remaining milk and simmer for another 45 minutes. Taste and season with salt and pepper. Add a little water or stock If the sauce becomes very thick during cooking.

4 Cook the pasta according to the packet instructions. Drain and toss in the oil. Cool a little, then arrange the shells in a large baking dish. Stuff with the bolognese sauce and bake in a preheated oven, 180°C/350°F, Gas 4, for 15 minutes. Serve with grated Parmesan, if using.

Cheese and tomato pizza

You'll be so, so popular! Pizza is one of those all time favorite teen foods, and is just right for friendly sleepover feasts.

Preparation 35 minutes, plus 1 hour, 10 minutes rising
Cooking 1 hour

4 cups (450g) strong bread flour
1 tsp salt
1 tsp dried mixed herbs
1 tbsp fast action dried yeast
oil, for greasing

For the topping:
1lb 12oz (800g) canned chopped
   tomatoes
4 tbsp tomato purée
2 garlic cloves, crushed
2 tsp sugar
1 cup (120g) cheese such as
   Cheddar or Emmental, grated
6 olives (optional)

1 Place the flour in a large bowl, add the salt, herbs, and dried yeast, then stir well. Add enough hand hot water, about 1–1½ cups (250–300ml), to form a smooth dough. Turn out onto a floured surface and knead the dough for 10 minutes.

2 Place the dough in a large, clean bowl that has been lightly brushed with oil. Leave in a warm place for about 1 hour until doubled in size.

3 For the topping: place the chopped tomatoes, tomato purée, garlic, and sugar in a large frying pan and bring the mixture to a boil. Reduce the heat and simmer for 40 minutes until thickened.

4 Roll out the dough into a rectangle, about 13 x 10in (33 x 26cm), and place on an oiled, flat baking sheet. Spread the tomato sauce over the dough, leaving a 2in (5cm) gap around the edge. Sprinkle over the cheese and olives, if using, and let rise in a warm place for 10 minutes.

5 Cook in a preheated oven, 220°C/425°F, Gas 7, for 20 minutes. Cut into squares and serve warm.

COOK'S TIP
This is a basic cheese and tomato version but you can add extra toppings—mushrooms, pepperoni, and ham all go down well.

Chocolate fondue with marshmallows

Guaranteed to keep 'em happy! Let them dip in and eat up. This is utterly irresistible and the easiest dessert to prepare.

Preparation 10 minutes   **Cooking** 5 minutes

1¹/₂ cups (375ml) heavy (double) cream
1 cup (250ml) milk
1 cup (225g) semisweet chocolate, roughly
  chopped
marshmallows, strawberries, chopped
  bananas, cubes of brioche, dates, for dipping

1 Pour the cream and milk into a saucepan or fondue bowl and bring to a boil. Turn off the heat and add the chocolate. Stir until the chocolate has melted and mixture is completely smooth.

2 Serve the chocolate warm with a selection of marshmallows, sliced fruits, and sweet breads.

COOK'S TIP
For a delicious alternative, replace the semisweet chocolate with the same quantity of chocolate caramel bar.

Mrs Emily Dewey's graduation dinner for Chuck Dewey

- Atlantic spiced salmon with new potato and scallion salad

- Roasted tomato and sour cream tarts

- Cobb salad

- Black cherry and chocolate cake

Serves 12

College graduation is an important milestone in every student's life; it is the gateway to the future, with all its hopeful promise of a happy and flourishing career. Moreover, every graduate who marches onto the podium to receive the magic certificate of success carries with them all the hopes and dreams of his or her proud parents.

Such pride is reflected here in Mrs Dewey's delightful menu for her son's graduation party. It is a thoughtful combination; there is grown-up elegance in the spiced salmon and the roasted tomato tart, of course. And there is also the affectionate gesture of including Chuck's favorite dessert—that irresistible Black Cherry and Chocolate cake. Mother really does know best!

This is an ideal menu to mark an important rite of passage occasion in a young person's life; it would be very suitable for an 18th birthday celebration, for example. It has just the right touch of formality to allow a brief interval for a 'good wishes' speech from a parent or a close family friend. Mostly, of course, it is created to celebrate and honor achievement—the major theme of every graduation party.

✔ Now is the time to invite the immediate family and close friends who have a great involvement in the new graduate's life.

✔ Take some time to search out some attractive invitations that reflect the new graduate's dignity and adult status.

✔ This is certainly not a sufficiently formal event to warrant sending engraved invitations. On the other hand, cartoon-type mortar boards and scrolls belong on congratulatory greeting cards, not on your invitations.

✔ The secret is to keep things simple. That way you won't go wrong, your son or daughter will feel at ease, and an important moment in family history will have been recorded with respect and joy.

Atlantic spiced salmon with new potato and scallion salad

Graduation day is an important event for momma too. Every proud mother wants to mark this important occasion, and this superb dish is a perfect choice.

Preparation 25 minutes, plus 2 hours marinating **Cooking** 40 minutes

12 Atlantic salmon fillets,
  about 8oz (225g) each
4 tbsp paprika
4 tbsp dried oregano
2 garlic cloves, crushed
1/2 tsp cayenne pepper
8 tbsp olive oil
salt and pepper

For the salad:
4 1/2 lb (2kg) new potatoes, scrubbed
10 tbsp oil
2 tbsp lemon juice
15 green (spring) onions, finely chopped
4 tbsp chopped fresh mint

1 Place the salmon fillets in a large nonmetallic dish. Mix together the paprika, oregano, garlic, cayenne, olive oil, and a few grinds of pepper. Pour the marinade over the salmon and work it into the flesh with your hands. Let marinate for 2 hours.

2 For the salad: cook the new potatoes in boiling salted water until tender. Mix together the oil and lemon juice. Drain the potatoes, then return them to the pan and pour the dressing over. Toss well, then cover and leave the potatoes to steep in the dressing for 30 minutes.

3 Meanwhile, place the salmon in a large roasting pan, season well with salt and roast in a preheated oven, 220°C/425°F, Gas 7, for 12–15 minutes. Set aside for 5 minutes before serving.

4 Transfer the potatoes to a serving dish and stir in the onions and mint.

COOK'S TIP
The salmon is best cooked briefly at a high temperature to retain its juiciness and flavor.

Roasted tomato and sour cream tarts

It's time to be a little more grown-up now, and these melt-in-the-mouth tarts certainly add a special touch of sophistication to the occasion.

Preparation 35 minutes, plus 1 hour chilling **Cooking** 2 hours, 45 minutes

20 large ripe tomatoes, halved
8 sprigs fresh thyme
4 3/4 cups (500g) all-purpose flour
2 1/4 cups (500g) very cold butter
2 1/2 cups (600g) sour cream
1 tbsp finely chopped fresh rosemary
1 cup (65g) fresh white bread crumbs
3/4 cup (55g) grated Parmesan

GIVE YOUR COOKING THE GOLDEN TOUCH

Bake-well

FOR PERFECT PASTRY

1 Place the tomatoes and thyme in a large roasting pan and cook in a preheated oven, 150°C/300°F, Gas 2, for 2 hours. Remove the thyme sprigs and let cool.

2 Place the flour and butter in a food processor and pulse 3–4 times—the butter should still be in fairly large lumps. Transfer to a bowl and add enough cold water, about 10 tbsp, to bring the mixture together. Cover in plastic wrap (cling film) and let chill for 30 minutes.

3 Roll out the dough into a long oblong. Fold the third of the dough closest to you up to the middle, and bring the top third down to overlap so it looks like an envelope.

4 Turn the dough 90° to the left so it now looks like a book, with the spine on the left. Roll out and repeat the folding twice more.

4 Divide the dough into 2 pieces. Roll out each piece to line two 8 x 11in (20 x 28cm) loose-bottomed tart pans. Let chill for 30 minutes.

5 Line the tart pans with baking paper and weigh down with baking beans. Bake in a preheated oven, 200°C/400°F, Gas 6, for 25 minutes. Remove the paper and beans and let dry in the oven for another 5 minutes.

6 Arrange the roasted tomato halves on the pastry. Drizzle the sour cream over and around the tomatoes. Mix together the rosemary, bread crumbs, and Parmesan and sprinkle over the tomatoes. Reduce the oven to 190°C/375°F, Gas 5, and bake for 20 minutes. Serve warm.

COOK'S TIP
This homemade puff pastry is delicious and surprisingly easy to make, but if you're desperate, you could use frozen.

Cobb salad

Hollywood's Brown Derby restaurant made this salad famous, so it's a great choice for your young graduation day star. Its full of different flavors and textures.

Preparation 25 minutes
Cooking 5 minutes

8oz (225g) cherry tomatoes, halved
12oz (350g) cucumber, roughly diced
6 Romaine lettuces, trimmed and roughly
  chopped
2 tbsp oil
8oz (225g) bacon, cut into thin pieces
5oz (150g) blue cheese, crumbled
20 black olives
4 hard-cooked eggs, quartered

For the dressing:
6 tbsp oil
1 tbsp white wine vinegar
1/2 tsp sugar
1/2 tsp mustard powder

1 Place the dressing ingredients in the bottom of a large salad bowl and whisk to amalgamate. Add the cherry tomatoes, cucumber, and lettuce but don't mix.

2 Heat the oil in a frying pan and cook the bacon for 5 minutes. Let cool a little, then spoon on top of the salad along with the cooking oil.

3 Add the blue cheese, olives, and hard-cooked eggs and mix everything together.

FRESH IDEA!

good seasons

SALAD DRESSING MIX

COOK'S TIP
Feel free to add whatever you have to hand for garnishes. Some crunchy croûtons or diced avocado would be fine additions.

Black cherry and chocolate cake

Enter this on the food roll of honor. The classic Black Forest Gateau graduates into this utterly enticing updated version.

Preparation 45 minutes, plus 1 1/2 hours chilling
Cooking 20 minutes

8 eggs
1 1/2 cups (175g) all-purpose flour, sifted
1/2 cup (55g) cocoa powder, plus extra for dusting
1lb 2oz (500g) fresh black cherries, pitted
8 tbsp cherry liqueur or dark rum
3 1/2 cups (800ml) heavy (double) cream
14oz (400g) semisweet chocolate, broken into pieces

1 Line two 10x12in (25X30cm) wide jelly (Swiss) roll pans with nonstick baking parchment. Put the eggs in a large mixing bowl, placed over a saucepan of simmering water. Beat with an electric whisk for about 15–20 minutes until very thick and pale. Remove from the heat and fold in the flour and cocoa.

2 Pour the mixture into the prepared pans and bake in a preheated oven, 200°C/400°F, Gas 6, for 12–15 minutes. Let cool.

3 Place the cherries in a bowl and pour the liqueur over. Heat the cream in a large saucepan. Place the chocolate in a large bowl and pour the hot cream over. Set aside for 5 minutes, then stir until completely smooth. Let chill for 45 minutes.

4 When the chocolate cream is cold, beat with an electric whisk for 5–10 minutes until thickened and pale.

5 Using a 10in (25cm) springform cake pan as a template, cut rounds out of the chocolate sponge. Line the bottom of the springform pan with one of the sponge disks. Arrange the cherries on top of the sponge, spooning half the liqueur over as well. Cover with three-quarters of the chocolate cream and top with the second sponge disk. Spread the remaining chocolate cream over the top and dust with cocoa powder. Let chill for at least 45 minutes before serving.

COOK'S TIP
You can make this cake at least 24 hours in advance, so you can get on with the rest of the menu. Remove it from the refrigerator 1 hour before serving.

Babe Walter's love you tender special

- Oysters gratinée
- Charbroiled Châteaubriand steak with herb béarnaise
- Deep-fried soufflé potatoes
- Iced summer berries with white chocolate sauce

Serves 2

Food and romance have always been closely entwined, and every woman knows this to be true, however much she tries to rationalize the secret dynamics of love. Consequently, with the right menu at her fingertips, she has real erotic power at her disposal when she cooks a meal designed to arouse the deeper passions of the man in her life.

The menu composed by Babe Walter touches all the right notes in the food/love repertoire. To begin with, there is the legendary aphrodisiac quality ascribed to oysters; and you must not forget that there is something utterly sensuous in the very act of swallowing these succulent morsels. Every woman should be aware of this fact, and know that her man's attention will already be alerted by this seductive start.

We are talking red-blooded males, here; and that simple fact is acknowledged by the inclusion of a prime cut of beefsteak in the menu—a superb châteaubriand, garnished with a luscious béarnaise sauce. Mmm! How can he resist? Well, make him wait a little, and enjoy sharing the delights of dipping ripe summer berries in a smooth chocolate coating. A pleasure for the mouth and for all the senses.

✔ Serve this seductive meal for two in a calm, dimly lit room; firelight would be perfect, of course, but candles can work their own enchantment. Use them to cast a soft, feminine light around the room.

✔ To boost the romantic ambience further, clear away every bit of clutter—you want his undivided attention.

✔ Put on his favorite smooch music—the sexier the better—he'll soon get the message.

✔ As for the dining table, show how special he is by bringing out your finest tablecloth, wine glasses, and silverware.

✔ You could also place a tiny bud vase in the center, with a single, scented flower such as a freesia or rose. But keep it simple—you don't want anything to prevent you gazing deeply into each other's eyes.

✔ Enjoy Babe Walter's menu and those 'love you tender' moments that keep romance alive however long you've been together.

Oysters gratinée

You want instant seduction? This easy yet incredibly sumptuous starter will signal your intentions with unerring accuracy. Oysters are high in zinc, hence their renown as an aphrodisiac. Serve simply with fresh, crusty bread to soak up the juices.

Preparation 15 minutes
Cooking 4 minutes

6 oysters, opened but still in
the shell
6 tbsp heavy (double) cream
2 tbsp grated Parmesan
2 tbsp fresh white bread
crumbs

1 Place the oysters in a heatproof dish. Spoon 1 tbsp of cream into each oyster shell. Mix the Parmesan with the bread crumbs and sprinkle the mixture over the oysters.

2 Broil (grill) under a preheated broiler (grill) for 3–4 minutes until golden and bubbling. Serve immediately.

Charbroiled Châteaubriand steak with herb béarnaise

Right, honey. Show your guy exactly how much you care with this classic French dish, with its luscious, sensuous béarnaise sauce. Serve with it a fresh green salad and deep-fried soufflé potatoes, (see below).

Preparation 10 minutes
Cooking 20 minutes

1 Châteaubriand steak, about 1lb (450g)
salt and pepper

For the béarnaise sauce:
2 egg yolks
1 stick (125g) chilled butter, cut into cubes
1 tsp white wine vinegar
1 tbsp chopped fresh tarragon

1 For the béarnaise sauce: place the egg yolks in a small bowl and heat over a saucepan of barely simmering water. Add the butter cube by cube, stirring well until the sauce amalgamates. Stir in the white wine and tarragon.

2 Remove the bowl from the heat and place in a large bowl half full of hot water to keep warm while you cook the steak.

3 Heat a charbroiler (grill) until it is very hot. Season the steak well and cook for 2–3 minutes per side or according to taste. Serve the steak with the béarnaise sauce.

COOK'S TIP
Don't make the béarnaise sauce too far ahead since the egg yolks are only partially cooked and they should not be kept warm for too long.

Deep-fried soufflé potatoes

These rich, crispy potatoes will melt in his mouth and can be made well in advance and deep-fried just before serving.

Preparation 20 minutes plus cooling **Cooking** 30 minutes

8oz (225g) potatoes
4 tbsp (55g) butter
2 tbsp milk
1/4 cup (25g) all-purpose flour
1 egg, beaten
oil, for deep-frying

1 Cook the potatoes until tender. Drain and mash with 2 tbsp (25g) butter and milk. Let cool.

2 Place 5 tbsp water and the remaining butter in a saucepan and heat gently until the butter has melted. Pour immediately into the flour and beat, off the heat, until smooth. Let cool. Beat in the eggs, and add the mixture to the potatoes.

3 Heat the oil for deep-frying until hot. Drop spoonfuls of the potato mixture into the oil and cook for 3–4 minutes until golden and puffed up. Lift out and drain on paper towels, then keep warm in the oven.

Iced summer berries with white chocolate sauce

Such a sweet idea, this. Each berry is like a mini ice lollipop, so you can enjoy them together as you gaze into each other's eyes. They are served smothered in a delicious, warm, creamy chocolate sauce.

Preparation 10 minutes, plus 45 minutes freezing **Cooking** 5 minutes

12oz (350g) mixed summer berries such as strawberries, blueberries, raspberries, blackberries
1 cup (250ml) heavy (double) cream
1 tsp vanilla extract
1/2 cup (75g) white chocolate, broken into pieces

1 Place the berries in a flat dish and freeze for 45 minutes.

2 Heat the cream and vanilla extract in a saucepan until it reaches boiling point. Add the chocolate and stir until melted and the sauce is smooth. Pour into a pitcher and serve warm with the iced berries.

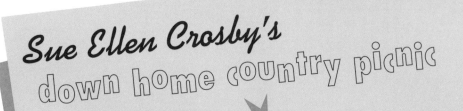

Sue Ellen Crosby's
down home country picnic

- **Tortilla wraps with honey roast ham and pepper** slaw

- **Spicy southern fried chicken with roasted corn salsa**

- **Tomato tart with Parmesan and cornmeal pastry**

- **Iced lemon and ginger cake**

Serves 8

It's hard to know why the very sight of the kitchen stove sometimes makes you long for the wide open spaces, but we all need to get out of that darned house from time to time. Maybe it's part of the good old pioneering spirit, but when the mood to head out for the country hits you, here's the perfect meal to take along. It's an old-fashioned down-home picnic party for you, your family, and friends. All your close folks.

The foods chosen by Sue Ellen Crosby for her special menu belong to the country heritage of the South. The flavors are great for fresh-air eating—there's nothing quite like the piquant contrast of earthy tortillas and chili-flavored fillings. As for the fried chicken, it is now one of the most popular dishes everywhere, and you couldn't chose anything nicer to eat on a picnic; it really is finger-licking good!

✔ The tomato tart and the ginger cake also make fine picnic food; they are easy to pack and carry, and you can cut them into neat slices so everyone has a share.

✔ Successful picnics don't happen on their own, of course—you need to check that you have everything you need before you set out. Oh, yes! Don't forget to pack a sharp knife; it makes life so much easier.

✔ Always make a list, and check off each item as you pack it. When you're miles away from home, there's no way that you're going to find salt and pepper in the middle of the woods—and it's surprising how many people forget to take these simple seasonings.

✔ If your picnic spot is near a running stream, put your bottles of wine and mineral water in a secure spot so they can keep cool.

✔ Sue Ellen's picnic will encourage you to get out of the house more, so you can breathe in some fresh air and get close to the land for a while. Then, when you get back, home will feel that little bit more special, after your spirit-lifting day in the great outdoors.

Tortilla wraps with honey roast ham and pepper slaw

Folks just love these tasty wraps, and they're easy to fix up on the spot, too. The pepper slaw has great flavor—sharp tang and richness combined.

Preparation 30 minutes

8 soft flour wraps
8 large slices honey roast ham
a few salad leaves

For the slaw:
1lb (450g) white cabbage, finely shredded
8oz (225g) carrots, grated
2 red bell peppers, seeded and finely sliced
1 cup (225g) mayonnaise
3/4 cup (175g) sour cream or plain yogurt
1 tsp white wine vinegar
salt and pepper

1 For the slaw: mix together the cabbage, carrots, and bell peppers in a large bowl. Mix the mayonnaise with the sour cream and vinegar, and season with salt and pepper.

2 Take 8 flour wraps and place a slice of ham in the top center of each one. Spoon 2–3 tbsp of the slaw on top with a few salad leaves. Bring up the bottom of the wrap and fold in the sides.

3 Secure each wrap with a toothpick and wrap in a napkin.

COOK'S TIP
You can also serve this slaw as an accompaniment to barbecued meats or hamburgers.

Southern fried chicken with roasted corn salsa

This is truly wonderful finger lickin' picnic food from way down South. The salsa is fairly hot stuff due to the chilies it contains, and may be too spicy for any juniors at the picnic. You may want to serve them the chicken on its own.

Preparation 40 minutes, plus 2 hours, 20 minutes marinating and cooling
Cooking 45 minutes

8 chicken thighs or drumsticks
2¹/₂ cups (600ml) milk
1 tbsp Tabasco or other hot sauce
1 cup (120g) all-purpose flour
1 tsp ground black pepper
1 tsp cayenne pepper
¹/₄ tsp salt
1 egg, beaten
2¹/₂ cups (450g) white vegetable shortening (white vegetable fat)

For the salsa:
3 corn cobs
1lb 5oz (600g) tomatoes, skinned, seeded, and diced
1 red chili, seeded and finely chopped
1 green chili, seeded and finely chopped
3 tbsp olive oil
1 tbsp chopped fresh parsley

1 Place the chicken pieces in a large saucepan, preferably in a single layer. Add the milk and hot sauce and let marinate for at least 2 hours.

2 Mix the flour with the pepper, cayenne pepper, and salt.

3 Bring the chicken to a boil, then reduce the heat and simmer for 20 minutes. Drain well, then pat dry and let cool for 20 minutes.

4 Dip the chicken pieces first in the seasoned flour, then the egg and then the flour again.

5 Heat the vegetable fat in a large frying pan until very hot. Add the chicken and cook for 4–5 minutes until golden brown. Drain on paper towels.

6 For the salsa: place the corn cobs on a charbroiler (grill) and broil (grill) for about 10 minutes, turning them frequently. Let cool, then with a sharp knife remove the kernels. Place the kernels in a bowl. Add the tomatoes with the chilies, oil, and parsley. Season well.

COOK'S TIP
Marinating the chicken in milk tenderizes the meat, so the longer you can leave it the better.

Tomato tart with Parmesan and cornmeal pastry

Here's something really special for a picnic feast. The cornmeal gives the pastry its extra bite and flavor, and contrasts beautifully with the light, rich cheesy filling.

Preparation 35 minutes, plus 30 minutes chilling
Cooking 1 hour, 10 minutes

2¼ cups (250g) all-purpose flour
½ cup (55g) fine cornmeal
¼ cup (25g) Parmesan, grated
½ cup (120g) butter
2 tbsp (25g) white vegetable shortening (white vegetable fat)
salt and pepper

For the filling:
4 tbsp (55g) butter
½ cup (55g) all-purpose flour
1⅔ cups (400ml) milk
½ cup (125ml) light (single) cream
½ cup (60g) Cheddar, grated
2 eggs
2 tbsp chopped fresh chives
3 tbsp Dijon mustard
4 ripe tomatoes, thinly sliced

1 Place the flour, cornmeal, Parmesan, butter, and shortening in a food processor. Add a pinch of salt and 4–5 tbsp cold water and process to a smooth dough. Cover in plastic wrap (cling film) and let chill for 30 minutes.

2 Roll out the pastry to line a 10in (25cm) tart pan. Line with baking paper and weigh down with beans. Bake in a preheated oven, 180°C/350°F, Gas 4, for 20–25 minutes until golden and crisp. Remove the baking paper and beans.

3 Melt the butter in a saucepan, stir in the flour, and cook for 2 minutes. Slowly pour in the milk, stirring well to make a smooth, thick sauce.

4 Stir in the cream and cook over a low heat for 2–3 minutes. Add the Cheddar, stir until melted, then let cool. Season well with salt and pepper. Beat in the eggs and chives.

5 Spread the mustard over the base of the pastry. Arrange three-quarters of the tomatoes over the mustard. Pour the cheese sauce over and arrange the remaining tomatoes on top.

6 Bake for 35–40 minutes until risen and slightly golden on top. Serve warm or cold.

Iced lemon and ginger cake

A homemade cake is an indispensable part of all good picnics, and this deliciously sticky, dark treat will have them all clamoring for more.

Preparation 30 minutes
Cooking 1 hour

2¼ cups (250g) all-purpose flour
2 tsp ground ginger
1 tsp ground cinnamon
2 tsp baking powder
pinch of salt
½ cup (120g) unsalted butter
½ cup (130g) soft brown sugar
1 cup (250ml) golden syrup
1 cup (250ml) black treacle
3 pieces crystallized stem ginger, finely
  chopped
½ cup (125ml) milk
2 eggs, beaten

For the icing:
2–3 tbsp lemon juice
1 cup (120g) confectioners' (icing) sugar, sifted

1 Mix the flour, ginger, cinnamon, baking powder, and salt in a large bowl.

2 Place the butter, sugar, syrup, and treacle in a saucepan and heat gently until melted. Beat it into the dry ingredients. Stir in the crystallized ginger and milk, then beat in the eggs.

3 Pour the mixture into a 8 x 10in (20 x 25cm) deep greased and bottom-lined cake pan. Bake in a preheated oven, 170°C/325°F, Gas 3, for 1 hour. Let cool before turning out.

4 For the icing: beat together the lemon juice and confectioners' sugar—it needs to be fairly thick so you may need to add extra confectioners' sugar to reach the required consistency. Pour the icing over the cake and let cool.

COOK'S TIP
This cake improves with age, so it is best to make it well in advance. You can serve it plain but the icing makes it that touch more special.

Mrs Ginger Bailey's
cowboy birthday beano

- Cowboy beans and sausages
- Potato wedges with melted cheese
- Vegetable crisps
- Baked Alaska birthday cake

Serves 8

The whole point about children's birthday parties is that they should be enormous fun. Kids grab any chance they get to whoop it up; and they also like using their imagination to transport themselves into a make-believe, vividly exciting experience. That's why junior and his friends simply adore dressing up as cowboys and cowgirls; it makes them feel that they're part of a colorful, classic icon; and that powerful, archetypal image is imprinted in most children's inner vision (probably through the ages of six to sixty!).

✔ No doubt about it, Ginger Bailey's menu is bound to be a great hit with rootin' tootin' youngsters everywhere. She has gone for no-nonsense, rib-sticking food, with hearty beans and sausages to keep energy levels high, and good-tasting vegetable crisps for delicious snacks. The high point of the menu, the Baked Alaska birthday cake, is an inspired choice; it's a special treat, something that everyone can enjoy.

✔ Remember, cowboy parties are supposed to be high-spirited affairs; so you'll have to expect plenty of "bang bang", swaggering, and tough guy talk.

✔ Keep the mood going with background music that they can sing along to—old cowboy favorites like "Home on the Range" and "A Four Legged Friend" go down well.

✔ The great thing about cowboy parties is that they have instant atmosphere; everyone knows what Westerns look like, and everyone can fit the part without getting it wrong.

✔ Have fun decorating the party venue with classic Western images; paste up "wanted" posters using blow-up photographs of your kids and their friends; draw pictures of giant cactuses; look up the internet to find classic motifs such as sheriff's stars, lassoes, spurs, saddles, six-guns, and stetson hats; in fact any image that speaks of the traditional West.

Cowboy beans and sausages

Ask your cowboy and cowgirl guests to holster their six-guns while they tuck into this chuck wagon special. These beans take a while to cook but are easy to prepare, resulting in a hearty, warming dish.

Preparation 20 minutes, plus overnight soaking
Cooking 4 hours, 20 minutes

2½ cups (450g) dried
  haricot beans
3 tbsp oil
2 onions, roughly chopped
2 garlic cloves, crushed
1½ cups (400g) canned
  chopped tomatoes
10oz (275g) smoked bacon,
  roughly chopped
1 tbsp black treacle
1 tbsp mustard powder
2 tbsp soft brown sugar
16 sausages
salt and pepper

1 Soak the beans overnight in plenty of cold water. Drain and place in a large saucepan. Cover with water, bring to a boil and boil for 15 minutes. Reduce the heat and simmer for 1 hour.

2 Meanwhile, heat the oil in a large casserole dish and cook the onions and garlic for 15 minutes. Add the tomatoes, bacon, treacle, mustard powder, and sugar and stir well.

3 Add the beans, cover, and cook in a preheated oven, 150°C/300°F, Gas 2, for 2 hours. Uncover and cook for another 1 hour.

4 Broil (grill) the sausages for 15 minutes, turning to ensure even cooking, then cut into bite-size pieces. Stir the bacon into the beans and cook for another 20 minutes. Taste and season with salt and pepper before serving.

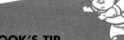

COOK'S TIP
For a speedy version, use 3x15oz (410g) cans haricot or cannellini beans instead of dried, and simmer for 1 hour.

Potato wedges with melted cheese

These potato wedges go down a treat, and are healthier and more satisfying than fries.

Preparation 20 minutes
Cooking 50 minutes

2lb 12oz (1.25kg) maincrop potatoes, halved, and cut into chunky wedges
1/2 cup (125ml) oil
2 cups (240g) Monterey Jack or Emmental cheese, grated
1/2 cup (125ml) heavy (double) cream

1 Place the potato wedges in a saucepan of salted water. Bring to a boil and simmer for 5 minutes. Drain well and arrange the potatoes in a single layer in a large roasting pan.

2 Pour the oil over, mix to coat the potatoes, and bake in a preheated oven, 200°C/400°F, Gas 6, for 40–45 minutes. Turn the potatoes once or twice during the roasting.

3 Place the cheese and cream in a nonstick pan and heat gently until the cheese has melted. Place the potatoes in a serving dish and pour the melted cheese over just before serving.

COOK'S TIP
If junior has more sophisticated tastebuds, substitute the Monterey Jack for a mild blue cheese.

Vegetable crisps

They're sweet, they're crunchy and especially popular with children. Carrots and celeriac can also be used to make great crisps.

Preparation 20 minutes
Cooking 40 minutes

1lb (450g) parsnips, peeled
1lb (450g) sweet potatoes, peeled
12oz (350g) beets, peeled
oil, for deep-frying

1 Slice the vegetables very finely in a food processor.

2 Heat the oil in a deep-fryer to 190°C/375°F. Cook each vegetable separately, a few at a time; 4–5 minutes for the parsnips, 5–6 minutes for the sweet potatoes and beets.

3 Drain on paper towels. Mix together the vegetable chips in a large bowl and serve.

Baked Alaska birthday cake

Dim the lights, and light the candles; it's the moment to sing the good old Happy Birthday song. This cake is an all-time favorite, but the fresh raspberries make it really special.

Preparation 50 minutes
Cooking 45 minutes

¾ cup (175g) unsalted butter

¾ cup (175g) granulated sugar

3 eggs, beaten

1 tsp vanilla extract

1½ cups (175g) self-rising flour, sifted

12oz (350g) raspberry jam

1½ cups (225g) raspberries

8 scoops vanilla or your favorite ice cream

4 egg whites

1 cup (225g) granulated sugar

candles or sparklers, to decorate

1 Cream the butter and sugar in a large mixing bowl. Add the eggs and vanilla extract and beat well. Fold in the flour. Spoon into a greased and bottom-lined 8in (20cm) cake pan.

2 Smooth the top of the mixture and cook in a preheated oven, 180°C/350°F, Gas 4, for 30–35 minutes or until risen and golden. Turn out and let cool on a wire rack.

3 Split the sponge in half horizontally. Place the bottom sponge on a baking sheet and spread with jam.

4 Place the second sponge disk on top. Arrange the raspberries on top of the sponge.

5 Place the egg whites in a large bowl and whisk until they form stiff peaks. Beat in the sugar, a spoonful at a time.

6 Place scoops of ice cream over the raspberries to cover. Spread the meringue mixture over the ice cream and sides of the sponge so everything is covered.

7 Cook in a preheated oven, 220°C/425°F, Gas 7, for 8–10 minutes. Remove from the oven, decorate with birthday candles or sparklers and serve immediately.

Martha Ferguson's Halloween party food

- Warm cheese and smoked chili dip with tortilla chips

- Chicken and sausage gumbo

- Pumpkin Pie

Serves 8

Martha Ferguson's Halloween party follows a time-honored tradition. On Halloween night, there's nothing like stoking up on good, hearty warming food to banish the wintry chill of the air, and get everyone in the mood for Trick or Treating expeditions. And there's no way that a real Halloween feast could be without a yummy pumpkin pie—just as there must be a nice, fat Jack–o'–lantern on the table, glowing through the darkness and frightening off any scary spirits and spooks wandering about. The custom of celebrating All Saints' Day and All Souls' Day which started at sundown on October 31 the night before, is very ancient. People originally believed that this was the night that all kinds of ghosts, spooks, vampires, and strange spirits roamed about the earth, and they had special ceremonies and rituals to protect themselves from these wayward beings.

Over the years, we have introduced our own cultural elements into the old festival; and it is now one of the most important celebrations in the calendar, for kids and adults alike. For children, dressing up in weird and wonderful costumes and Trick-or-Treating door to door is still the main event. In the fifties, costumes were homemade, and kids invented amazing devil outfits, ghost get-ups and witch or wizard attire from simple items in the dressing-up box. Now, of course, the stores pile their shelves with a wide range of ghoulish costumes to satisfy all tastes.

✔ If you would like people to dress up for your Halloween party, let them know on the invitation, so they have plenty of time to choose an outfit in advance. You can have fun with the invitation and make it as spooky as you want—anything goes on Halloween!

✔ The major theme for the night is anything connected with the supernatural—this applies to everything from your party outfit to the Halloween decor. You'll run into witches with broomsticks, wizards, skulls, vampires, and ghosts all around your neighborhood, so don't be surprised.

✔ Some people still like to have traditional games such as apple bobbing at their Halloween parties; it's something that kids and adults both enjoy, so it's a good idea to have a special corner set aside for this activity.

✔ Finally, remember that Trick-or-Treating isn't just for juniors—why not grab some goodie bags, join the kids on their expeditions—and recapture the magic of your own childhood?

Warm cheese and smoked chili dip with tortilla chips

There may be a slight nip in the air at Halloween, so the chipotle chilies in this spicy flavored dip are just the thing to warm you up. Dip in there and enjoy the night's adventures.

Preparation 15 minutes
Cooking 20 minutes

4 soft wheat tortillas, cut into triangles
oil, for deep-frying

For the dip:
1 tbsp butter
5 green (spring) onions, finely chopped
1 chipotle (smoked) chili, soaked in hot
  water for 20 minutes
1¼ cups (300ml) heavy (double) cream
2½ cups (300g) Monterey Jack cheese,
  grated

1 Heat the oil to 190°C/375°F and cook the tortillas for 2–3 minutes. Drain on paper towels.

2 Melt the butter in a saucepan and cook the onions for 5 minutes.

3 Drain the chipotle chili and finely chop. Stir the chili into the onions, then add the cream and cheese. Cook over a low heat until the cheese has melted. Serve warm with the tortilla chips to dip.

COOK'S TIP
Chipotles are smoked, medium-hot jalapeño chilies—you can substitute a milder dried chili, if preferred, or if you can't find chipotles.

Chicken and sausage gumbo

You'll love this warming, hearty dish—it's perfect food to set you up for Trick-or-treating. Serve the gumbo with plain rice and fried okra.

Preparation 35 minutes
Cooking 1 hour, 5 minutes

3 tbsp light olive oil
12oz (350g) smoked sausage, cut into 1/4 in (5mm) slices
2lb (900g) chicken thighs, cut in half
1 onion, finely chopped
2 sticks celery, finely sliced
2 garlic cloves, crushed
1 green bell pepper, seeded and finely chopped
2 tbsp all-purpose flour
14oz (400g) canned chopped tomatoes
1 3/4 cups (450ml) chicken stock
2 tbsp chopped fresh parsley
gumbo filé (optional)
salt and pepper

1 Heat 2 tbsp oil in a large casserole dish and brown the sausage slices for 3–4 minutes. Remove with a slotted spoon and set aside.

2 Add the chicken pieces and brown, a few at a time, for 3–4 minutes. Remove with a slotted spoon and combine with the sausage.

3 Pour the remaining oil into the casserole and add the onion, celery, garlic, and bell pepper. Cook, stirring to prevent them burning, for 10 minutes. Stir in the flour and cook for another 5 minutes.

4 Add the tomatoes and chicken stock, and bring to a boil. Add the sausage and chicken, stir well, and season with salt and pepper. Cover and simmer gently for 40 minutes. Check the seasoning and just before serving stir in the parsley and sprinkle over the filé, if using.

COOK'S TIP
Gumbo filé is a powder made from the dried leaves of the sassafras tree and is a staple ingredient in Cajun and Creole cuisine.

Pumpkin Pie

Nope! You simply can't have Halloween without pumpkins. The sweet flesh is the main ingredient of this sweet, spicy tart. It tastes best served warm with very cold light (single) cream.

Preparation 25 minutes
Cooking 55 minutes

1 pre-baked 12in (30cm) pastry case

For the filling:
2lb (900g) pumpkin to yield 1¹/₂lb (675g)
 pumpkin pulp, flesh cut into 2in (5cm) pieces
2 eggs, beaten
¹/₃ cup (90g) soft brown sugar
1 cup (250ml) golden syrup
1 cup (250ml) heavy (double) cream
2 tsp ground cinnamon
1 tsp ground ginger
¹/₂ tsp ground nutmeg
1 tsp vanilla extract

1 Place the pumpkin in a saucepan and cover with water. Bring to a boil, then simmer for 15 minutes until tender. Drain the pumpkin very well, cool and purée in a blender or food processor. Spoon into a large mixing bowl.

2 Add the eggs, sugar, golden syrup, and cream to the pumpkin purée and mix well. Stir in the spices and vanilla extract. Spoon the mixture into the pastry shell and bake in a preheated oven, 190°C/375°F, Gas 5, for 30–35 minutes until the filling is firm to the touch. Serve warm with cold light (single) cream.

COOK'S TIP
You should use the hollowed out pumpkin to make a traditional halloween lantern.

Mrs Joanne Wiley's
celebration summer barbecue

- **Sticky ribs**

- **Beefburgers**

- **Cornmeal muffins**

- **New potato and crispy bacon salad**

- **Vanilla terrine with summer berry compote**

Serves 8

Everyone enjoys a celebratory barbecue feast in the summer. All over the world, people gather together for traditional festivities. These may be large community affairs (where a whole ox may be roasted over an open fire) or, more often, a home barbecue for friends and neighbors.

This is what Joanne Wiley has chosen for her special menu; and it certainly does reflect all the best qualities of outdoor eating, with its friendliness and relaxed informality. Beefburgers have effectively become an universal dish, as have barbecued ribs; so there's nothing more popular that you can serve up for your hungry guests! This is hearty food that everyone can enjoy; and barbecues are great for getting folks together in an easy manner. Guests will also enjoy the crispy bacon flavors in the potato salad, and the summer fruits in the terrine have that hint of vanilla to put people in a great, mellow mood.

✔ Barbecues are very relaxed, fun occasions so you can really go to town with your design themes. Creative folk will enjoy sending out unusual invitations to echo the party style. For instance, if you're hosting an 'old time' event, and know how to use a calligraphy pen, try writing your invitations on rough-edged parchment, for an authentic 'rustic' look. Roll each one up, secure it with raffia, and send out in a small tube mailer.

✔ As for the color scheme; the sky's the limit. It's a good idea to stick to a few, strong, simple colors, however. But use your imagination, and interpret this in different ways; for instance, try floating different colored candles in large, shallow bowls or galvanized pails.

✔ Thread rows of colored fairy lights along your porch or patio deck—they also look great strung amongst trees and shrubs in the garden.

✔ Shop around your local gift stores for brightly colored paper napkins, plates, knives, forks, and plastic cups to match your color scheme; and arrange them in groups of colors for contrast.

✔ Finally, if you like flowers, you may like to decorate your main serving table with a bunch of colorful, fresh, blooms, arranged in a simple, rustic pitcher. A delightful finishing touch

Sticky ribs

There's nothing like the informality of a barbecue to get everyone in a friendly frame of mind—guests simply can't stand on ceremony while they're getting stuck into these succulent ribs. Just hand them plenty of paper napkins, and watch the fun.

Preparation 15 minutes
Cooking 2 hours, 10 minutes

2lb 12oz (1.25kg) pork ribs
1/2 cup (125ml) soy sauce
3 garlic cloves, crushed
3/4 cup(175g) sugar
1/2 cup (115g) tomato ketchup
1 tsp ground ginger

1 Place the pork ribs in a large saucepan and cover with 2 1/2 pt (1.5lt) water. Add the soy sauce, garlic, sugar, tomato ketchup, and ginger. Bring to a boil, then reduce the heat and simmer for 1 1/4 hours.

2 Remove the ribs from the saucepan, leaving the cooking stock. Increase the heat and boil the liquid for 30 minutes, until it has reduced to a thick and sticky sauce.

3 Place the ribs in a large roasting pan, pour the sauce over, making sure the ribs are covered.

4 Broil (grill) the ribs over hot coals for 8–10 minutes, turning them halfway through cooking and brushing with the sticky marinade.

COOK'S TIP
The ribs can be prepared up to the end of step 3 at least 24 hours in advance. You can also roast the ribs in a hot oven for 20–25 minutes, if preferred.

Beefburgers

Hoorah. Here come the burgers. These have a strong claim to being everyone's favorite dish, so let's celebrate their popularity. Serve in a bun with pickles and relish.

Preparation 20 minutes, plus 30 minutes chilling
Cooking 25 minutes

2 tbsp oil
1 onion, finely chopped
2 garlic cloves, finely chopped
2lb 4oz (1kg) ground beef
1 tsp dried thyme
1 tsp dried parsley
1 tsp Worcestershire sauce
salt and pepper

1 Heat the oil in a frying pan and cook the onion and garlic for 10 minutes until softened. Let cool.

2 Place the beef, thyme, parsley, and Worcestershire sauce in a large mixing bowl. Season well with salt and pepper. Stir in the onion and garlic mixture.

3 Divide the mixture into 8 and shape into patties. Place on waxed paper and let chill for 30 minutes.

4 Broil (grill) the beefburgers over very hot coals for 10–15 minutes and serve.

COOK'S TIP
Homemade beefburgers are easy to make; they are extra good when made with top quality ground beef— so buy the best you can afford.

Cornmeal muffins

Mmm, how delicious. These muffins are light and fragrant and really are at their best eaten fresh from the oven.

Preparation 15 minutes **Cooking** 25 minutes

3 cups (350g) all-purpose flour
1½ cups (145g) cornmeal
2 tsp baking powder
1 tsp salt
2 tsp mustard powder
3 tbsp chopped fresh chives
4 tbsp (55g) butter, melted
2 eggs, beaten
1 cup (250g) buttermilk
1 cup (250ml) milk

1 Place the flour, cornmeal, baking powder, salt, mustard powder, and chives in a large mixing bowl. Make a well in the center.

2 Mix together the butter, eggs, buttermilk, and milk and pour into the well. Stir until everything is just mixed together—don't over mix or the muffins will be heavy.

3 Spoon into 12 muffin paper cases in a muffin pan. Bake in a preheated oven, 200°C/400°F, Gas 6, for 20–25 minutes.

New potato and crispy bacon salad

Your guests will love this classy salad, and rightly so, as it is composed from lovely, tasty ingredients.

Preparation 15 minutes **Cooking** 50 minutes

2lb 4oz (1kg) small new potatoes, scrubbed
10oz (275g) asparagus spears, woody stalks
  removed
6 garlic cloves, unpeeled
6 tbsp oil
7oz (200g) streaky bacon
½ cup (225g) blue cheese, crumbled
2 tbsp chopped fresh parsley
1 tbsp chopped fresh chives
salt and pepper

1 Place the new potatoes in a saucepan of salted water. Bring to a boil and cook for 5 minutes. Drain and place in a roasting pan with the asparagus and garlic cloves. Season with salt and pepper and drizzle with oil. Roast in a preheated oven, 200°C/400°F, Gas 6, for 45 minutes.

2 Meanwhile, lay the bacon in a roasting pan and cook in the oven for 10–15 minutes until brown and crispy. Remove and let cool. Crumble the bacon into small pieces.

3 Once the potatoes are cooked discard the garlic cloves. Put the potatoes in a serving dish with the asparagus, set aside until just warm, then scatter with the bacon, blue cheese, and herbs. Serve warm or cold.

COOK'S TIP
The new potatoes
and asparagus are
roasted to concentrate
their flavor.

Vanilla terrine with summer berry compote

Wow your guests with this stunning summer dish—the cream, vanilla, and summer fruit are a perfect partnership.

Preparation 30 minutes, plus 5 hours chilling
Cooking 5 minutes

3 egg yolks
1 cup (120g) confectioners' (icing) sugar
1 vanilla bean, split down the middle
1 tsp vanilla extract
5 leaves gelatin or 1 tbsp
  granulated gelatin
2 cups (500ml) heavy (double) cream

For the compote:
9oz (250g) raspberries
1²/3 cups (250g) blackberries
2 cups (225g) blueberries
7oz (200g) strawberries, hulled and halved
1¹/3 cups (55g) confectioners' (icing) sugar,
  sifted

1 Place the egg yolks in a bowl with the sugar. Scrape out the vanilla seeds with the tip of a knife and add to the egg yolks with the vanilla extract; whisk until light and fluffy.

2 Soak the gelatin in 4 tbsp water for 5 minutes. Place in a small saucepan and melt over a low heat. Stir the gelatin into the egg yolk mixture.

3 Lightly whisk the cream until it begins to leave a trail. Fold it into the egg yolk mixture. Pour into a 2pt (1.2lt) loaf pan lined with plastic wrap (cling film.) Let chill for at least 5 hours.

4 For the compote: place the raspberries, blackberries, blueberries, and strawberries in a large saucepan. Add the sugar and cook over a low heat for 5 minutes or until the juices of the fruit start to run. Let cool before serving.

5 Turn the terrine out onto a long dish and serve in slices, with the compote on the side.

COOK'S TIP
If liked, add a couple of tablespoons of crème de cassis to the compote.

classy canapé parties

Mitzi Johnson's
canapé party favorites

- Louisiana crabcakes with dipping sauce

- Tuna melts

- Smoked salmon pinwheels

- Marinated shrimp with dill mayonnaise

- Lamb meatballs with buttermilk and herb dip

- Pigs in blankets

- Deep-fried garlic mushrooms

- Angels on horseback

- Spicy fish croquettes

- New England fishballs

- Creamy onion and Monterey Jack tartlets

- Spicy charbroiled chicken bites

- Herby popovers with blue cheese

- Roast beef on crispy potatoes with horseradish cream

- Mint cooler

- Lime zinger

- Sparkling fizz

There's nothing quite so thrilling as giving a successful canapé party. This is the moment to show off your skills as a spell-binding hostess. Everyone needs a little magic in their lives—so here's your chance to dress up in your most glitzy outfit, and create a great 'happening' buzz for your friends.

Mitzi Johnson's special canapés are a hit with her guests on two major counts; they are satisfyingly substantial and deliciously tasty, so her guests never leave her party desperate for something nice to eat.

✔ **The retro touch** While you're expressing your genius for bringing everyone together for a glittering hour or two, it's reassuring to know that these classic 1950s canapés have never been more popular. That's because they're all thoroughly tried and tested, so everyone can relax and concentrate on having a good time. We've also included some non-alcoholic 'cocktails' for those who don't drink but want to blend in with the scene.

✔ **Timing** In less frantic times, the typical canapé party ran from between 6pm to 8pm; nowadays, as people work later into the evening, you'll find it easier to hold the event a little later; or you could make the party briefer; a maximum of 1½ hours, perhaps.

✔ **Be specific** Whatever you decide, make sure that you mention the exact time that the party begins and ends on your invitation; many of your guests will want to go on to other events such as dinner or theater, so they need to know the schedule.

✔ **Look your best** You need to feel that you're in control of the occasion, so take off your apron, hide your cooking tools and get yourself dressed up and ready for action at least fifteen minutes before you're expecting your first guests.

✔ **Set the mood** Run your eye over the party room to ensure that everything is welcoming and stylish. Now you can light the candles, turn on the music and let the fun begin.

✔ **Get people talking** As your guests arrive, take their coats and get them drinks immediately. Introduce them to people who are already there.

✔ **Brilliant delegating** If you're hostessing on your own, it's a good idea to ask your most sociable friends to help you with breaking the ice and getting people talking together. They'll be pleased to help. Having something to do at a party puts everyone at ease, so don't be shy about asking your pals to mix up a batch of drinks while you hand around some of your delicious canapés.

✔ **Your reward** At some point into the party, some mysterious alchemy happens. All around the room you'll suddenly notice people smiling and becoming marvellously witty. That means you've done it. You've put together a truly happy hour (or two) right here in your own home, and people will leave with memories of what a wonderful hostess you are. Congratulations!

Louisiana crabcakes with dipping sauce

An appetizingly spicy nibble, these crabcakes are extremely rich so they're ideal served in bite-size morsels. Your guests will love them.

Preparation 20 minutes, plus 30 minutes chilling **Cooking** 15 minutes

1lb (450g) white and brown crabmeat
1 cup (55g) fresh white bread crumbs
½ cup (115g) mayonnaise
3 scallions, finely chopped
1 large red chili, seeded and finely chopped
2 tbsp chopped fresh cilantro (coriander)
oil, for frying
seasoned flour, for dusting
salt and pepper

For the dipping sauce:
2 tomatoes, skinned, seeded, and finely chopped
1 cup (250ml) tomato ketchup
1 shallot, very finely chopped
¼ tsp dried Cajun spice mix

1 Mix together all the ingredients for the crabcakes. Taste and season with salt and pepper. Shape into about 40 small cakes and let chill for 30 minutes.

2 For the dipping sauce: mix the tomato with the remaining ingredients and set aside.

3 Heat a little oil in a nonstick skillet. Dip the crabcakes in the seasoned flour and cook for 1–2 minutes each side until golden. Serve the crabcakes with the dipping sauce on the side.

Makes about 40

Tuna melts

Hands will appear from everywhere to pick up these delicious little bites of melting tuna and cheese.

Preparation 40 minutes **Cooking** 15 minutes

20 slices white bread
5 tbsp (75g) butter, melted
14oz (400g) canned tuna in oil, drained
  and flaked
$\frac{1}{2}$ cup (115g) mayonnaise
2 tbsp chopped fresh chives
grated peel of 2 lemons
1 cup (120g) Cheddar cheese, grated
salt and pepper

1 Cut out rounds of bread with a 2$\frac{1}{2}$ in (6cm) pastry cutter to make 40 croûtes—you should get 2 rounds per slice of bread. (Use the off-cuts to make bread crumbs.)

2 Lay the bread rounds on a baking sheet and brush with melted butter. Bake in a preheated oven, 180°C/350°F, Gas 4, for 10 minutes until crisp and golden.

3 Mix the tuna with the remaining ingredients. Taste and season with salt and pepper. Place 1 heaped tsp of the tuna mixture on each croûte, making sure you spread the mixture to the edges of the bread so it doesn't burn when broiled.

4 Place the croûtes on to a baking sheet and broil (grill) for 2–3 minutes until slightly brown and just beginning to melt. Serve warm.

COOK'S TIP
These can be made well in advance and cooked just before serving.

Makes about 40

Smoked salmon pinwheels

A classy hostess knows her all time classics, and these are still amongst the most popular canapés in town. Serve them with confidence.

Preparation 20 minutes

6 slices brown bread, crusts removed
1 cup (225g) cream cheese
1 tbsp mayonnaise
1 tbsp chopped fresh dill
5oz (150g) smoked salmon slices
pepper
fresh dill, to garnish

1 Lay the bread on a board and flatten slightly with a rolling pin.

2 Beat the cream cheese with the mayonnaise and dill. Spread the mixture thinly over the bread. Arrange the salmon on top to cover the cream cheese and trim any overlapping pieces with a sharp knife. Season with pepper.

3 Roll up each slice of bread, starting from the longest side, and cut into 6 or 7 slices. Garnish with dill.

Makes about 40

Marinated shrimp with dill mayonnaise

These are a real party treat, and your guests will be delighted that you've gone to so much trouble to please them. Juicy large shrimp (prawns) are made extra succulent when dipped into the lavish dill mayonnaise.

Preparation 25 minutes, plus 1 hour marinating
Cooking 10 minutes

40 large raw peeled shrimp (prawns)
2 garlic cloves, crushed
juice and grated peel of 2 limes
1 red chili, seeded and very finely chopped

For the dill mayonnaise:

2 egg yolks
1 tsp mustard powder
2 tsp white wine vinegar
pinch of salt
1 cup (250ml) peanut or vegetable oil
2 tsp sour cream
1 tbsp chopped fresh dill
salt

1 Place the shrimp (prawns) in a shallow, nonmetallic dish. Mix together the garlic, lime juice, peel, and chili. Pour the marinade over the shrimp (prawns). Mix well and marinate for 1 hour.

2 To make the mayonnaise: place the egg yolks, mustard powder, vinegar, and salt in a mixing bowl. Using an electric whisk, beat in the oil, drop by drop at first. When half of the oil has been added, pour in the remaining oil in a thin, steady stream, whisking continuously. If the mayonnaise becomes very thick, dilute with 1 tbsp warm water.

3 Stir the sour cream and dill into the mayonnaise. Let chill until ready to serve.

4 Place the shrimp (prawns) in a steamer (you may need to do this in batches) and steam for 3–4 minutes until they turn pink and firm. Serve chilled or at room temperature with the dill mayonnaise.

Makes 40

COOK'S TIP
Don't be tempted to substitute inferior small shrimp (prawns) for the larger variety, which are far tastier.

Lamb meatballs with buttermilk and herb dip

A delicate hint of the east. These mini Moroccan meatballs are full of warm, spicy flavor, while the dip makes the perfect cooling, tangy accompaniment.

Preparation 30 minutes plus 30 minutes cooling **Cooking** 25 minutes

3 tbsp oil, plus extra for frying
2 onions, finely chopped
4 garlic cloves, crushed
2 tbsp paprika
2 tsp dried thyme
2 tsp cinnamon
2lb (900g) ground lamb
2 tbsp finely chopped fresh cilantro
* (coriander)*
salt and pepper

For the buttermilk dip:
1¼ cups (300ml) buttermilk
1 tsp chopped fresh thyme
1 tbsp chopped fresh chives

1 Heat the oil in a large frying pan and cook the onions and garlic for 10 minutes. Add the paprika, thyme, and cinnamon and cook for another 1–2 minutes. Let cool completely.

2 Mix the onion mixture into the lamb, then add the cilantro (coriander), and season well with salt and pepper. (To test the level of seasoning, cook a nugget of the mixture.)

3 Shape the mixture into 40 small meatballs. Heat a little oil in a large frying pan and cook the meatballs for 10–12 minutes, turning them halfway through cooking.

4 For the dip: mix together the buttermilk and herbs. Taste and season with salt and pepper.

5 Serve the meatballs warm with toothpicks for your guests to dunk the meatballs into the buttermilk dip.

Makes about 40

COOK'S TIP
The meatballs can be made well in advance and heated through before serving.

Pigs in blankets

Yes, they're fine old favorites and, yes, they taste good. That's why you like to serve them at your parties. But what a difference homemade flaky pastry and good quality sausagemeat makes.

Preparation 35 minutes, plus 1 hour chilling and 30 minutes freezing
Cooking 20 minutes

1½ cups (350g) butter
4 cups (450g) strong bread flour
pinch of salt
1lb 12oz (800g) good quality sausages or sausagemeat
2 eggs, beaten

1 Place the butter in the freezer for 30 minutes. Sift the flour and salt into a large mixing bowl. Grate the frozen butter into the flour, then mix in with a narrow spatula—don't use your hands since the heat from them will soften the butter.

2 Add 6–7 tbsp cold water to the flour or enough to bring the mixture together into a dough. Cover in plastic wrap (cling film) and chill for 1 hour.

3 Divide the pastry into 4 pieces. Roll each piece into a 13 x 6in (33 x 15cm) rectangle.

4 Remove the skins from the sausages, divide them between the pastry, and lay them down the center of each piece, joining the ends to form one large sausage. If you're using sausagemeat, divide it into 4 equal parts to make each large sausage

5 Fold the top of the pastry over the sausagemeat and brush with beaten egg. Fold over the bottom of the pastry and press down to seal. Turn the sausage roll over so that the join is underneath. Brush the surface with more beaten egg. Repeat with the other pieces of pastry.

6 Cut each sausage roll into about 12. Bake in a preheated oven, 220°C/425°F, Gas 7, for 20 minutes until golden. Serve warm.

Makes about 48

HERB
Party Snack

Deep-fried garlic mushrooms

Thank heaven for mushrooms. They were just made for finger-food ideas. These are delicious on their own or with a herby dip.

Preparation 30 minutes
Cooking 20 minutes

1lb 2oz (500g) small cap mushrooms,
  about 30
1/2 cup (120g) butter
2 garlic cloves, crushed
2 tbsp chopped fresh parsley
1/3 cup (75g) all-purpose flour
2 eggs, beaten
3 1/2 cups (225g) dried bread crumbs
oil, for deep frying

1 Remove the stalks from the mushrooms. (You can use them to make stock.) Beat the butter with the garlic and parsley.

2 Stuff the mixture into the mushroom cavities. Dip each mushroom into the flour, then the egg, and then the bread crumbs.

3 Heat the oil in a deep fryer until hot—a cube of bread dropped in the oil should sizzle immediately and brown in about 20–30 seconds. Deep-fry the mushrooms, a handful at a time, for 4–5 minutes and keep warm.

Makes about 30

COOK'S TIP
You can prepare these mushrooms well in advance and cook them just before serving.

Angels on horseback

Get your glittering party going with these all-time classic canapés; you know that they are a delicious treat and a must for a successful party.

Preparation 50 minutes
Cooking 10 minutes

15 thin slices unsmoked streaky bacon
30 oysters, shucked

1 Cut each slice of bacon in half across the centre, so you have 30 short pieces.

2 Lay a piece of bacon on a board and place an oyster at one end. Roll up the bacon and place on a baking sheet, join end down. Repeat with the remaining bacon and oysters.

3 Place under a preheated broiler (grill) and broil (grill) for 10 minutes or until the bacon is golden all over. Serve warm with toothpicks.

COOK'S TIP
For an alternative version, substitute the oysters for pitted prunes to make devils on horseback.

Spicy fish croquettes

Fresh salmon, herbs, and chilies are bound together in a thick béchamel and fried until crisp.

Preparation 40 minutes, plus 45 minutes chilling **Cooking** 20 minutes

1½lb (675g) cooked salmon fillet, skinned
4 tbsp (55g) butter
1 tsp mustard powder
½ cup (55g) flour
¾ cup (185ml) milk
2 egg yolks
5 green (spring) onions, finely chopped
2 tbsp chopped fresh cilantro (coriander)
2 red chilies, seeded and finely chopped
4 cups (250g) dried bread crumbs
1 tsp dried Cajun spice mix
oil, for frying
salt and pepper

1 Flake the salmon into a large mixing bowl. Melt the butter in a saucepan, add the mustard powder and flour and cook, stirring, for 2 minutes. Gradually add the milk and cook for 2–3 minutes, stirring until smooth.

2 Taste and season with salt and pepper, then set aside the béchamel until completely cold. Beat in the egg yolks once cold.

3 Mix the onions, cilantro (coriander), and chilies into the flaked salmon, then stir in the cold béchamel. With slightly damp hands, shape the mixture into small croquettes.

4 Mix the bread crumbs with the Cajun spice, and dip each croquette into the bread crumbs. Let chill for 30 minutes.

5 Heat some oil in a frying pan and cook the croquettes for 6–7 minutes, turning to ensure they are evenly brown. Serve warm.

> **COOK'S TIP**
> These can also be served as a main course—simply make 12 large croquettes.

Makes about 30

New England fishballs

A regional delicacy, these small, light fishballs should be served hot with maybe a tartare sauce for dipping.

Preparation 15 minutes, plus 30 minutes chilling
Cooking 20 minutes

Makes about 25

2 tbsp oil, plus extra for frying
1 onion, finely chopped
1lb 6oz (640g) cod fillet, roughly chopped
1 tbsp chopped fresh tarragon
1 tbsp chopped fresh parsley
grated peel of 1 lemon
¼ cup (60ml) heavy (double) cream
1 egg

1 Heat the oil in a frying pan over a medium heat and cook the onion for 10 minutes until softened and just golden. Set aside until cold.

2 Place the onion, cod and remaining ingredients in a food processor and process until well mixed.

3 Shape the fish mixture into walnut-size balls and let chill for 30 minutes.

4 Heat a little oil in a frying pan and cook the fishballs for 3–4 minutes each side until golden.

COOK'S TIP
For an easy tartare sauce dip, simply mix some chopped cornichons, a handful of chopped capers and chopped parsley with a good quality mayonnaise.

Creamy onion and Monterey Jack tartlets

Miniature tartlets are just the thing for parties—and these are especially popular, as they simply melt in the mouth.

Preparation 40 minutes, plus 15 minutes cooling **Cooking** 45 minutes

*double quantity of shortcrust pastry recipe
  (see Mushroom and Bacon Tart, page 55)
4 tbsp (55g) butter
2 tbsp oil
2 cups (450g) onions, finely chopped
1 tsp chopped fresh thyme
1 cup (120g) Monterey Jack cheese or
  Cheddar, grated
½ cup (125ml) heavy (double) cream
salt and pepper*

1 Make the pastry following the instructions on page 55. Roll out the pastry, stamp out 36 x 2in (5cm) diameter rounds and line mini muffin pans with the pastry disks—you may have to do this in batches if you don't have enough pans.

2 Melt the butter and oil in a large frying pan. Add the onions and thyme and cook gently for 30 minutes until the onions are very soft and light golden. Let cool for 15 minutes.

3 Place 1 tsp onion in the bottom of each tartlet. Spoon 1 tsp cream on top, and sprinkle with 1 tsp cheese and some pepper.

4 Bake the tartlets in a preheated oven, 190°C/375°F, Gas 5, for 20 minutes. Let rest in the pan for 2–3 minutes, then lift the tartlets out and serve warm or cold.

Makes about 36

COOK'S TIP
These tartlets taste best fresh and warm from the oven, but you can make them at least 24 hours in advance and simply heat them through.

Spicy charbroiled chicken bites

Folks just love these tasty little bites, so make sure you make plenty to offer around. They'll be coming back for more.

Makes about 40

Preparation 20 minutes, plus 2 hours marinating **Cooking** 30 minutes

6 skinless chicken breasts,
  cut into bite-size pieces
3 garlic cloves, crushed
1 cup (250ml) buttermilk
2 tsp medium or hot curry powder
  1 tbsp tomato purée
  2 tbsp chopped cilantro (coriander)
salt and pepper

1 Place the chicken in a nonmetallic dish.

2 Mix together the garlic, buttermilk, curry powder, and tomato purée. Season with salt and pepper. Pour the marinade over the chicken pieces and mix well to coat. Cover and let chill for at least 2 hours or overnight.

3 Heat a charbroiler (grill) until it is very hot—you may need to lightly oil it. Remove the chicken from the marinade and charbroil (grill) a few pieces at a time for 4–5 minutes each side. Sprinkle the chicken with the cilantro (coriander) and serve warm or cold with toothpicks.

COOK'S TIP
These also make a great sandwich filler or can be finely chopped into a pasta salad.

Herby popovers with blue cheese

Canapé parties are light hearted occasions and demand easy, delicious morsels. Popovers are airy clouds of herby batter, which, here, have a melted cheese center.

Preparation 20 minutes
Cooking 25 minutes

1¼ cups (145g) all-purpose flour
½ tsp salt
1¼ cups (300ml) milk
2 eggs, beaten
1 tbsp oil
2 tbsp chopped fresh chives
1 tbsp chopped fresh parsley
3oz (75g) blue cheese, cut into small cubes

1 Place the flour in a large bowl and stir in the salt.

2 Mix the eggs with the oil and herbs, then gradually beat the mixture into the flour.

3 Grease 2 x 12-bun mini muffin pans. Fill each muffin hole with the batter until about three-quarters full. Place a cube of cheese in the center of each one.

4 Bake in a preheated oven, 220°C/425°F, Gas 7, for 12–15 minutes until puffed up and golden. Reduce the heat to 180°C/350°F, Gas 4, and cook for another 5–8 minutes.

COOK'S TIP
Make the batter in advance and cook the popovers an hour before the party, that way they will stay light and fresh.

Makes 24

Roast beef on crispy potatoes with horseradish cream

Very special, you will be popular.

Preparation 45 minutes, plus overnight chilling
Cooking 45 minutes

1½ lb (675g) fillet of beef
4 medium-sized potatoes
oil, for shallow frying
3 tsp grated fresh horseradish
1 cup (250g) sour cream
1 tbsp chopped fresh chives, plus extra to
  garnish
salt and pepper

1 Roast the beef in a preheated oven, 220°C/425°F, Gas 7, for 25 minutes. Let cool, then chill, preferably overnight—this will make the beef easier to slice thinly.

2 Thinly slice the potatoes, about 1/16 in (2mm) thick, using the slicing blade of a food processor, discarding the end pieces, which will be too small. (The potatoes shouldn't be quite as thin as a potato fry.)

3 Heat the oil in a large frying pan and cook the potato slices in small batches for 4–5 minutes each side until crisp and golden. Drain on paper towels and lay on a baking sheet.

4 Mix the horseradish with the sour cream and chives, and season well with salt and pepper. (The dip will thicken up after a few minutes.) Cut the beef into very fine slices, then cut into thin strips.

5 To serve, pile a few slivers of beef on top of each potato crisp. Top with 1 tsp horseradish cream and garnish with chives.

Makes about 30

COOK'S TIP
The secret to the success of this canapé is to use very crisp potatoes and very rare beef so it is meltingly tender.

Mint cooler

Imagine yourself as a glamorous belle from the Deep South as you savor this delightfully refreshing party drink

20 sprigs fresh mint
8 tsp granulated sugar
2 tbsp lemon juice
2 cups (500ml) dry ginger ale
8 cups crushed ice
mint leaves, to decorate

1 Remove the mint leaves from the stalks and place in a pitcher with the sugar, lemon juice, and ginger ale. Mix together, slightly crushing the mint leaves. Fill 8 glasses with the crushed ice and pour over the mixture. Garnish with mint leaves.

Serves 8

Lime zinger

**Lime adds an extra-special citrus zip to
the pineapple base of this great tasting
'mocktail'. Enjoy!**

3 limes
½ cup (125ml) pineapple juice
2 tbsp granulated sugar
2 cups crushed ice

1 Grate the peel of 1 lime into a cocktail shaker.
Squeeze the juice from all the limes and add to the
shaker. Stir in the pineapple juice and sugar, add
the ice and shake well. Dip the rims of the glasses
into a little lime juice, then sugar, if liked, before
filling with the drink.

Serves 2

Sparkling fizz

Serve this fizz in elegant Champagne flutes for sophisticated presentation.

6 sugar lumps
6 tbsp grenadine
4 cups (1lt) dry ginger ale, chilled

1 Place a sugar lump in the bottom of each Champagne flute. Working quickly, pour over 1 tbsp grenadine and top up with ginger ale.

Serves 6

friendly coffee mornings

Hope Granger's
morning coffee selection

- Oatmeal and raisin cookies
- Chocolate sandwich cookies
- Cupcakes
- Cherry strudel
- Cinnamon swirl teabread
- Gooey chocolate cake
- Blueberry angel food cake
- Molasses and gingerbread

- Emmental and roasted corn spoon bread
- Bacon and caramelized onion rolls
- Hot chocolate
- Ice cream soda
- Homemade lemonade

Coffee mornings were immensely popular social events during the 1950s, and every hostess worth her salt (and pinafore) had her personal repertoire of delicious baked goodies. Many recipes were handed down from mother to daughter, and the tradition of inviting folks over for a morning break lasted through decades. What sweet aromas infused these occasions—the cinnamon-scented aromas of newly baked cakes and fresh coffee filled the air, and everything looked so pretty! It was an ideal opportunity for the proud hostess to bring out her best coffee (or tea) set, and display her cakes on delicate lace-edged doilies.

✔ There's still a lot to be gained from continuing these simple traditions, even though they seem part of a long-lost era. Coffee mornings are friendly, informal ways of keeping friends and neighbors in touch. They don't take up hours of the day, and you can bake your choice of recipes well ahead of time.

✔ While it is now quite unusual for most people to have time to spare for daytime entertaining, working patterns are becoming more flexible. Those who work from home often feel left out of social networks and would welcome a friendly get-together for coffee and cakes.

✔ On a practical level, holding coffee mornings has always been an effective way of raising money for charities and community projects. The proceeds from the sale of freshly baked cakes have contributed generous funds to an untold number of good causes.

✔ If you want to host a coffee morning at your home, you can create a wide variety of menus from Hope Granger's favorite selection. Her recipes are all delicious, but much depends on how much time you have available. If you're really busy, stick to the quickly made cookies and cupcakes, and treat your guests to a more ambitious homemade teabread or strudel on another occasion.

✔ Morning coffee occasions needn't be rigid affairs; for instance, many people prefer drinking tea, so always have it on hand as an alternative. You may also like to offer other refreshments such as Ice Cream Soda and Homemade Lemonade.

✔ This is your chance to show off your treasures. Rather than keeping your pretty china and table linen hidden away in the cupboard, take this opportunity to put them on display. You can often find the most exquisite hand-embroidered table cloths in thrift stores, and these set off your table beautifully.

✔ Polish up your silver coffee spoons, get out your best coffee (or tea) pot, and prepare to enjoy a relaxed, friendly hour at the beginning of the day that you can share with like-minded friends.

129

Oatmeal and raisin cookies

Invisible hands will be raiding your cookie jar to steal these fruity, oaty bakes. They're come-back-for-more treats, and so easy to make.

Preparation 20 minutes
Cooking 20 minutes

1 cup (225g) rolled oats
1¾ cups (200g) self-rising flour
1 cup (175g) raisins
1 cup (225g) unsalted butter
1¼ cups (275g) soft brown sugar
2 eggs, beaten

1 Mix together the rolled oats, flour, and raisins in a bowl.

2 Beat together the butter and sugar until light and creamy. Add the eggs gradually, beating well. Stir in the oat mixture until everything is combined.

3 Take 2 tbsp of the cookie dough and shape into a round. Place on a nonstick cookie sheet and flatten slightly. Continue with the rest of the dough leaving about 4in (10cm) between each cookie.

4 Bake in a preheated oven, 180°C/350°F, Gas 4, for 20 minutes until golden. Let cool for 5 minutes before transferring the cookies to a wire rack.

Makes 12 large cookies

Chocolate sandwich cookies

Here's a pretty contrast—the dark richness of the cocoa cookies is tempered by the mellow flavor of the vanilla buttercream filling.

Preparation 15 minutes plus 30 minutes cooling
Cooking 20 minutes

1 cup (225g) unsalted butter
½ cup (120g) granulated sugar
2½ cups (275g) self-rising flour
½ cup (55g) cocoa powder
2 tbsp milk

For the filling:
4oz (115g) butter
4oz (115g) confectioners' sugar, sifted
1 tsp vanilla extract

1 Cream the butter and sugar in a bowl until light and creamy. Sift in the flour and cocoa powder, then add the milk and mix everything together.

2 With slightly damp hands, shape the dough into walnut-sized balls. Place on a greased cookie sheet and press down with the back of a fork.

3 Bake in a preheated oven, 180°C/350°F, Gas 4, for 15–20 minutes. Let cool on a wire rack.

4 For the filling: beat the butter, sugar, and vanilla extract together until smooth and creamy. Once the biscuits are cold, spread a little butter icing on the flat base and sandwich together.

Makes 24 cookies
(12 sandwich cookies)

Cupcakes

A touch of sweet nostalgia—the maple syrup gives these cupcakes a deliciously different flavor and combines wonderfully with the cream cheese frosting.

Preparation 25 minutes
Cooking 15 minutes

For the frosting:

¾ cup (185g) cream cheese
4 tbsp (55g) unsalted butter, softened
1¾ cups (225g) confectioners' sugar, sifted
1 tsp vanilla extract

For the cupcakes:

½ cup (120g) unsalted butter, softened
1 cup (250ml) maple syrup
2 eggs, beaten
1¾ cups (200g) self-rising flour

Makes 14 small cupcakes

1 For the frosting: beat the cream cheese with the softened butter until smooth. Add the confectioners' sugar and vanilla extract and beat until smooth. Chill for 30 minutes.

2 Meanwhile, line a muffin pan with 14 paper muffin cases. For the cupcakes: beat the butter until soft and creamy. Gradually add the maple syrup, beating well to incorporate it into the butter. Beat in the eggs and fold in the flour.

3 Spoon 1 heaped tbsp of the batter into each muffin case. Bake in a preheated oven, 180°C/350°F, Gas 4, for 15 minutes or until risen and golden. Let cool before spreading the frosting generously over the cakes.

Cherry strudel

Soft and luscious, this traditional favorite will have folks dropping by on all kinds of pretexts. But, as the hostess with the mostess, you'll know exactly what they really want...

Preparation 40 minutes
Cooking 25 minutes

1lb 4oz (550g) fresh black cherries, pitted and halved
¼ cup (40g) ground almonds
⅓ cup (90g) granulated sugar
1 cup (55g) fresh cake crumbs
4 large sheets filo pastry
4 tbsp (55g) unsalted butter, melted
confectioners' sugar, for dusting

1 Place the cherries in a bowl with the ground almonds, granulated sugar, and cake crumbs, then stir to combine.

2 Cover the filo pastry with a damp cloth to prevent it drying out. Lay a sheet of the pastry on a large flat baking sheet and brush with a little melted butter. Lay a second sheet over the top and brush with butter. Repeat this twice more so you have a rectangle of 4 sheets of pastry.

3 Spoon the cherry mixture over the top, leaving a gap of 2in (5cm) around the edge. Roll up the longest side—like you would a jelly (Swiss) roll. Tuck in the ends and form into a horseshoe shape.

4 Brush the surface of the pastry with more butter and bake in a preheated oven, 190°C/375°F, Gas 5, for 25 minutes. Dust with confectioners' sugar and serve warm or at room temperature.

Serves 8

COOK'S TIP
The cherries must be dark and ripe for the best flavor—you could use canned cherries but make sure they are well drained. If you don't have a homemade sponge, a store bought Madeira cake is ideal for the cake crumbs.

Cinnamon swirl teabread

Your reputation as a generous hostess will be greatly enhanced with this rich, spice-scented bread. Serve it with your favorite brand of tea.

Preparation 20 minutes, plus 1 hour, 15 minutes rising **Cooking** 30 minutes

6½ cups (750g) strong white flour
½ cup (120g) granulated sugar
1 tsp salt
2 tbsp (25g) fast action dried yeast
½ cup (120g) unsalted butter
1⅔ cups (400ml) milk
2 eggs, beaten
4 heaped tbsp soft brown sugar
2 tsp ground cinnamon

1 Place the flour, granulated sugar, and salt in a large mixing bowl. Stir in the dried yeast. Make a well in the center of the flour.

2 Melt the butter in a saucepan. Pour in the milk and heat until it is just hand hot. Pour the mixture into the well in the flour, add the eggs and mix everything together with a wooden spoon until you have a smooth, very soft dough.

3 Cover the dough and let rise in a warm place for 45–60 minutes until it has doubled in size. Mix the soft brown sugar with the cinnamon.

4 Beat the dough with a wooden spoon to knock back or deflate. With well floured hands, divide the dough into 4 pieces. Butter a 4pt (2.4lt) kugelhopf mold or 2 x 2pt (1.2lt) loaf pans.

5 Place a piece of dough in the mold and stretch it round the bottom until it is covered. Sprinkle over a quarter of the cinnamon sugar mixture. Take a second piece of dough and stretch it over the first one. Sprinkle with cinnamon sugar. Repeat twice more. Let rise for 15 minutes.

6 Bake in a preheated oven, 220°C/425°F, Gas 7, for 20 minutes. Reduce the oven to 190°C/375°F, Gas 5 and cook the bread for another 5–10 minutes. Turn out onto a wire rack and let cool.

COOK'S TIP
This teabread is more like a brioche, which is why it needs extra yeast to help it rise. Here, it is baked in a kugelhopf mold but you could use 2 loaf pans, if preferred.

Serves 10–12

Gooey chocolate cake

Sheer, outrageous indulgence. How can they resist? The sponge makes this cake deliciously gooey and melt-in-the-mouth.

Preparation 35 minutes
Cooking 45 minutes

11oz (300g) semisweet chocolate, at least 70% cocoa solids
¾ cup(175g) unsalted butter
8 eggs, separated
1 cup (200g) soft brown sugar
½ cup (55g) ground almonds

For the frosting:
⅔ cup (150g) unsalted butter
1¾ cups (225g) confectioners' sugar, sifted
¼ cup (40g) cocoa powder, sifted

1 Grease and line the bottom of a 8in (20cm) springform cake pan, then line the sides with aluminum foil.

2 Melt the chocolate and butter in a large bowl, placed over a saucepan of gently simmering water. Let cool.

3 Beat the egg yolks with the sugar until thick and pale. Stir in the cool chocolate and butter mixture, then the ground almonds.

4 Whisk the egg whites until they form soft peaks. Fold them into the chocolate mixture. Pour into the prepared cake pan. Place the pan in a roasting pan half full of hot water.

5 Bake in a preheated oven, 180°C/350°F, Gas 4, for 40–45 minutes until the cake is quite firm but a skewer inserted into the center comes out a little messy. Let cool in the pan, then transfer the cake to a plate.

6 For the frosting: melt the butter in a pan. Add the confectioners' sugar and cocoa powder and beat well. Add 1–2 tbsp hot water and beat until glossy. Chill for 15 minutes or until the frosting has a spreadable consistency. Spread the frosting over the top and sides of the cake.

Serves 8–10

COOK'S TIP
Try not to overcook the cake mixture—it is better slightly undercooked.

Blueberry angel food cake

Your visitors will think you're an angel yourself when you serve this gossamer light cake. It's dotted with plump blueberries and topped with whipped cream and more blueberries.

Preparation 30 minutes
Cooking 40 minutes

7 egg whites
1 tsp vanilla extract
1 tsp cream of tartar
1¼ cups (275g) granulated sugar
1½ cups (175g) all-purpose flour, sifted
2½ cups (275g) fresh blueberries
1 cup (250ml) half-and-half (whipping cream)
confectioners' sugar, for dusting

1 Grease and line the bottom of an 8in (20cm) springform cake pan.

2 Whisk the egg whites with the vanilla extract until foamy. Add the cream of tartar and whisk until the egg whites form soft peaks.

3 Gradually add the sugar, whisking until the egg whites are stiff. Add the flour and fold in. Finally fold in half of the blueberries.

4 Spoon the mixture into the prepared cake pan. Bake in a preheated oven, 170°C/325°F, Gas 3, for 35–40 minutes or until a skewer inserted into the center comes out clean. Let cool in the pan, then loosen the sides and transfer the cake to a plate.

5 Whisk the cream until stiff and spread it over the top of the cake. Scatter with the remaining blueberries and dust with confectioners' sugar just before serving.

Serves 8–10

Molasses and gingerbread

Everyone will enjoy this afternoon treat—it's really a hybrid of a cake and a teabread and is delicious served sliced with unsalted butter.

Preparation 25 minutes
Cooking 1 hour, 15 minutes

3½ cups (400g) all-purpose flour
1 tsp baking powder
1 tbsp ground ginger
1 tsp ground cinnamon
1 cup (225g) unsalted butter
½ cup (125g) dark molasses
¾ cup (175g) soft brown sugar
3 eggs
3oz (75g) glacé cherries, halved
4oz (115g) chopped dried dates
2oz (55g) stem ginger
¾ cup (90g) sultanas

1 Grease and line a 8½in (21cm) square cake pan.

2 Mix together the flour, baking powder, ground ginger, and cinnamon in a large bowl.

3 Place the butter in a saucepan with the molasses and brown sugar. and stir over a low heat until melted. Pour it into the flour mixture and mix well. Beat in the eggs and stir in the remaining ingredients.

4 Pour the mixture into the prepared cake pan and bake in a preheated oven, 150°C, 300°F, Gas 2, for 1–1¼ hours, or until a skewer inserted into the center comes out clean. Turn out onto a wire rack and let cool.

Serves 8–10

Emmental and roasted corn spoon bread

This cornmeal dish is a variation on a traditional favorite. Try it for yourself—you'll find that it's as delicious as the original.

Preparation 20 minutes
Cooking 1 hour, 15 minutes

3 corn cobs
3 tbsp oil
1 cup (120g) all-purpose flour
1½ cups (150g) cornmeal
1 tbsp baking powder
½ tsp baking soda
½ tsp salt
2 eggs
1 cup (250ml) buttermilk
4 tbsp (55g) butter, melted
½ cup (55g) Emmental cheese, grated

1 Place the corn cobs in a roasting pan and pour over the oil. Roast in a preheated oven, 200°C/400°F, Gas 6, for 30 minutes. Let cool, then slice off the kernels—you should have about 4 oz (115g).

2 Mix together the flour, cornmeal, baking powder, baking soda, and salt in a large bowl.

3 Add the eggs and buttermilk and beat well. Stir in the melted butter, Emmental, and corn kernels.

4 Spoon into a 2pt (1.2lt) greased and lined loaf pan. Bake in a preheated oven, 190°C/375°F, Gas 5, for 40–45 minutes or until a skewer inserted into the center comes out clean. Set aside for 10 minutes before turning out onto a wire rack. Serve just warm.

Serves 6–8

COOK'S TIP
This has a firmer texture than a true spoon bread, which means it is cooked in a loaf tin and sliced.

138 *Hostess with the Mostess*

Bacon and caramelized onion rolls

Fill your home with the aroma and flavor of freshly baked bread—there is truly nothing better. These savory rolls are delicious filled with smoked salmon and watercress, cream cheese and chives, or just plain with a pat of butter.

Preparation 45 minutes, plus 1 hour, 20 minutes rising **Cooking** 50 minutes

Makes 12 rolls

2 tbsp (25g) butter
1 onion, finely chopped
1 tsp sugar
1 tbsp oil, plus extra for brushing
4oz (115g) lean bacon, finely chopped

For the dough:
4½ cups (500g) strong plain flour
1 tsp salt
2 tsp (10g) fast action dried yeast
1¼ cups (300ml) milk
1 egg, beaten

1 Melt the butter in a frying pan. Add the onion and sugar and cook over a low heat for 25–30 minutes until the onion is deep golden. Remove and let cool.

2 Add the oil and bacon to the frying pan and cook for 5 minutes. Mix the bacon with the onion and set aside until completely cold.

3 Place the flour in a large bowl and stir in the salt and yeast. Heat the milk until it is just hand hot and pour it into the flour. Add the egg, and onion and bacon, then mix together. Turn the dough out onto a well-floured board and knead for 10 minutes. Place the dough in a clean, oiled bowl, cover and let rise for 1 hour.

4 Knock back the dough with your fist to deflate, then divide it into 12 even pieces. Knead each piece of dough for 2 minutes, then shape into a roll.

5 Place the rolls on a large baking sheet and brush with oil. Let rise for another 20 minutes until doubled in size and bake in a preheated oven, 220°C/425°F, Gas 7, for 10–15 minutes until golden.

6 Remove the rolls from the oven and cover with a damp dish towel until cold—this will give the rolls a soft crust.

Homemade drinks

Hot chocolate

Wrap yourself around with this comforting, warming drink; it's a real luxury, especially when made with good quality semisweet chocolate and whole milk. For extra indulgence, place a spoonful of whipped cream on top of each mug.

Preparation 5 minutes
Cooking 2 minutes

2½ cups (600ml) whole milk
2 cinnamon sticks
5oz (150g) semisweet chocolate, at least 70% cocoa solids, broken into pieces
½ cup (125ml) heavy (double) cream, whipped (optional)

1 Place the milk with the cinnamon sticks in a saucepan and bring to a boil. Remove from the heat and add the chocolate; stir until melted.

2 Remove the cinnamon sticks and pour the hot chocolate into 4 mugs. Top each one with 1 tbsp whipped cream, if using, and serve immediately.

Serves 4

Hot Chocolate

Fixed in seconds . . . superb in flavor
—with Baker's Instant!
2-3 heaping teaspoons Baker's Instant
One cup hot milk

Put Baker's Instant in cup; stir in hot milk gradually.
(A marshmallow adds a marvelous touch.) That's
all you do for the best hot chocolate drink you ever
tasted. Truly delicious cocoa, with the unmatched
flavor of Walter Baker chocolate—finest in the world.

Baker's Instant makes a superb cold chocolate milk
too—instantly! Treat yourself to the best—be sure
to get Baker's Instant!

Ice cream soda

You don't have to kick your heels at the soda fountain to get in the mood for fun. Vanilla ice cream soda is one of the best but you can choose your favorite ice cream to create your own flavor combinations.

Preparation 5 minutes

8 scoops good quality ice cream
4 tbsp heavy (double) cream
4 cups (1lt) cream soda or plain soda
fresh raspberries, to garnish

1 Place 2 scoops ice cream in each glass. Spoon 1 tbsp of cream over the ice cream. Pour in the cream or plain soda and top with raspberries.

Homemade lemonade

All summer long, keep pitchers of this refreshing, zingy thirst quencher in your refrigerator.

Preparation 10 minutes

4 unwaxed lemons, quartered
3/4 cup (175g) granulated sugar
6 1/4 cups (1.5lt) water
ice cubes and lemon slices, to serve

1 Place the lemons in a blender or food processor with the sugar and 1 1/4 cups (300ml) water. Process for a few seconds until the lemons are finely chopped.

2 Pour the mixture through a strainer. Add the remaining water and stir well. Add ice cubes and a few extra lemon slices before serving.

Index

Picture Credits

Look! Conversion tables

P.S. only use one system at a time!

Liquid Measures

¼ tsp	=	1.25ml
½ tsp	=	2.5ml
1 tsp	=	5ml
2 tsp	=	10ml
1 tbsp	=	15ml
2 fl oz	=	60ml
4 fl oz	=	125ml
5 fl oz	=	150ml
6 fl oz	=	185ml
8 fl oz	=	250ml
½ pt	=	300ml
13 fl oz	=	375ml
14 fl oz	=	400ml
¾ pt	=	450ml
18 fl oz	=	500ml
1 pt	=	600ml
1¼ pints	=	750ml
1¾ pints	=	1 litre
2 pints	=	1.2 litres
2½ pints	=	1.5 litres
3½ pints	=	2 litres

Dry Measures

¼oz	=	10g	8oz	=	225g
½oz	=	15g	9oz	=	250g
¾oz	=	20g	10oz	=	275g
1oz	=	25g	11oz	=	300g
1½oz	=	40g	12oz	=	350g
2oz	=	50g	14oz	=	400g
2½oz	=	65g	15oz	=	425g
3oz	=	75g	1lb	=	450g
3½oz	=	90g	1¼lb	=	500g
4oz	=	115g	1½lb	=	675g
4½oz	=	130g	2lb	=	900g
5oz	=	150g	2¼lb	=	1kg
5½oz	=	165g	3–3½lb	=	1.5kg
6oz	=	175g	4–4½lb	=	1.75kg
6½oz	=	185g	5–5¼lb	=	2.25kg
7oz	=	200g	6lb	=	2.75kg

Butter

			⅓ cup	=	75g
			½ cup	=	120g
1 tbsp	=	15g	⅔ cup	=	150g
2 tbsp	=	25g	¾ cup	=	175g
3 tbsp	=	45g	1 cup	=	225g
4 tbsp	=	55g	1½ cups	=	350g
5 tbsp	=	75g	1 stick	=	115g
6 tbsp	=	90g	1½ sticks	=	175g
			3 sticks	=	350g